NATURAL WONDERS

WATERFALLS

75 MOST MAGNIFICENT WATERFALLS

AN OCEANA BOOK

This book is produced by
Oceana Books
6 Blundell Street
London
N7 9BH

ISBN-13: 978-1-84573-402-2

QUMWATER

Editor: Richard Wiles
Designer: Kevin Collier
Picture Researcher: Ildikó Egervári
Contributors: Ian Penberthy, Amy Head &
Deborah Hercun

Printed in Singapore by
Star Standard Industries (Pte) Ltd.

NATURAL WONDERS

WATERFALLS

75 MOST MAGNIFICENT WATERFALLS

George Lewis

Oceana

CONTENTS

Captivating cascades

A waterfall is usually a geological formation resulting from water, often in the form of a stream, flowing over an erosion-resistant rock formation that forms a sudden break in elevation.

Some waterfalls form in mountain environments where erosion is rapid and stream courses may be subject to sudden and catastrophic change. In such cases, the waterfall may not be the end product of many years of water action over a region, but rather the result of relatively sudden geological processes such as landslides, faults or volcanic action.

Typically, a stream flowing across an area will form shelves across the streamway, elevated above the further stream bed when the less erosion-resistant rock around it disappears. Over a period of years, the edges of this shelf will gradually break away and the waterfall will steadily retreat upstream, creating a gorge. Often, the rock stratum just below the more resistant shelf will be of a softer type, causing undercutting. Splashback creates a shallow cave-like "rock shelter," under and behind the waterfall.

Eventually, the outcropping, more resistant cap rock will collapse under pressure to add blocks of rock to the base of the waterfall. These blocks of rock are then broken down into smaller boulders by attrition as they collide with each other, and they also erode the base of the waterfall by abrasion, creating a deep plunge pool.

Waterfalls can also form due to glaciation, whereby a stream or river flowing into a glacier continues to flow into a valley after the glacier has receded or melted.

Streams become wider and more shallow just above waterfalls due to the flow over the rock shelf, and there is usually a deep pool just below the waterfall due to the kinetic energy of the water hitting the bottom.

Far left: *Waterfalls have always been a magnet for people, and many of the world's most magnificent have viewing areas. Many of the 275 tiers and segments of Iguaçu Falls, on the border of Brazil and Argentina, are served by walkways that allow viewers to get close to the gushing waters. At one point a person can be surrounded by 260 degrees of waterfalls.*

Top right: *The 2,648ft (807m) freefalling plunge of the mighty Angel Falls in Venezuela is the longest in the world. Buffeted by high winds the water is turned to mist before reaching the base. Reaching the base of the falls is arduous, but this spectacular view is witnessed from nearby Raton Island.*

Above right: *More accessible than the remote Angel Falls, Niagara Falls—straddling the Canadian and U.S. border—is a major tourist draw. It consists of two main parts, the Horseshoe Falls on the Canadian side, and the American Falls (shown) on the U.S. side, a block formation 1,060ft (323 m) wide.*

Right: *Iceland's Gullfoss has a broad, block formation, which descends in three steps, only to plunge into a deep crevice that runs at right angles to the flow of the river Hvítá. A viewing area allows visitors to survey the spectacle at close quarters.*

Right: *Without a point of visual reference, it is often difficult to appreciate the sheer scale of the world's spectacular waterfalls. This arresting image reveals the essence of man's relationship to the waterfall, as figures at the base of India's mighty Jog Falls appear like ants.*

Types of waterfalls

Block:	Water descends from a relatively wide stream or river.
Cascade:	Water descends a series of rock steps.
Cataract:	A large waterfall.
Fan:	Water spreads horizontally as it descends while remaining in contact with bedrock.
Horsetail:	Descending water maintains some contact with bedrock.
Plunge:	Water descends vertically, losing its contact with the bedrock surface.
Punchbowl:	Water descends in a constricted form, then spreads out in a wider pool.
Segmented:	Distinctly separate flows of water form as it descends.
Tiered:	Water drops in a series of distinct steps or falls.
Multi-Step:	A series of waterfalls one after another of roughly the same size each with its own sunken plunge pool.

Bridalveil Falls

Yosemite National Park, California, USA

- **Bridalveil Falls is 620ft (189m) tall, plunging directly into Yosemite Valley.**
- **It is one of the few falls in Yosemite to run all year, fed mostly by snow runoff flowing down Bridalveil Creek, whose source is Ostrander Lake.**
- **Bridalveil is only a modest 40ft (12m) wide, which suggest the appearance of a wispy veil that gives the falls its name.**

Bridalveil Falls is perhaps the most scenic spot in the majestic Yosemite National Park, and is one of the most famous waterfalls in the USA. The Ahwahneechee called the area Pohono, "Spirit of the Puffing Wind," capturing the delicate swirling spray of the falls. It appears slight, blowing sideways when the wind takes it, but it is a powerful waterfall, as tall as a 60-story building. When the flow is very weak during the summer, it is possible to swim at the broad base of the falls, but the force of water from such a height can still drive a person under.

Yosemite Valley was carved by glaciers that left many "hanging valleys"—where the tributary valleys are higher than the main valleys that it flows into. With the sole exception of Bridalveil, all of the waterways that fed the other waterfalls carved the hanging valleys into steep cascades.

Yosemite National Park is a UNESCO World Heritage Site, and is visited by 3.5 million visitors a year, most of whom rarely venture farther than the Yosemite Valley. It covers an area of 1,189 square miles (3,081km), nearly all of which is designated a wilderness zone. The park is famous for its outstanding natural beauty and its biodiversity. The most popular place to view the falls is from the overlook on Wawona Road. From the darkness of the tunnel, the marvel of the valley and its falls suddenly burst into view.

Far left: *The falls plunge off the imposing sheer granite cliffs of Cathedral Rocks, which stand some 6,630ft (2,021m) high. The stark white streak of the descending waters give the falls its evocative name.*

Top right: *In the spring, even from a distance of a few hundred yards, the visitor to Bridalveil Falls will still find themselves drenched by the spray from the plunging water.*

Right: *This panoramic view from Yosemite National Park's seventy-four year old Wawona Tunnel greets travelers as they emerge into daylight. The broad sweep of the valley lies before them, with Bridalveil Falls a prominent feature beneath the towering Cathedral Rocks.*

DISCOVERY OF A TREASURE

The first Europeans to see the falls were probably members of a troop organized by the state of California, the Mariposa Battalion, which was formed to protect the interests of gold miners in Sierra Nevada who were reportedly under attack from the local indigenous tribe. In 1851, one such expedition brought them to Yosemite Valley. The grandeur of the landscape overwhelmed the group. Lafayette Bunnel suggested the name of Yosemite, though he mistakenly believed it was the native name. Though his original purpose was not one of exploration, Bunnel became a key figure in the "discovery" of Yosemite.

Yosemite National Park, USA

Lake Taho
Sacramento
San Francisco
Salinas
Fresno

Bridalveil Falls, Yosemite National Park

Cheonjeyeon Waterfall

Seogwipo, Jeju Island, South Korea

- **Cheonjeyeon Waterfall is a spectacular three-tier cascade, near the city of Seogwipo, in the south of Jeju Island, South Korea.**

- **The fall's name means "Pond of the Heaven's Emperor," and refers to a legend of nymphs, who descended from heaven at night to bathe in the pool.**

- **Cheonjeyeon Waterfall is more than just a tourist site to the people of Jeju. Since ancient times it has been thought that standing under the waterfall on certain special days can cure diseases.**

Roughly oval-shaped, Jeju Island measures 40 miles (64km) from east to west and 16 miles (26km) from north to south. At its center is Mount Halla, an extinct volcano 6,398ft (1,950m) tall that now contains a lake in its main crater.

The whole of Cheju shows signs of ancient volcanic activity. Inland, there are hundreds of hills that were the sides of craters, and the coast is characterized by cliffs that mark the point where the lava was suddenly cooled and solidified by contact with the sea.

Since the end of the last Ice Age, Jeju's fresh water has had to find its way to the sea over these steep and hard formations, thus creating numerous waterfalls, of which Cheonjeyeon is one of the most impressive.

Located to the west of Jungmnun village the east of Saekdal-ri, Cheonjeyeon is named in the memory of a legend that tells of seven beautiful nymphs, assistants to the Heaven's Emperor, who would come down to Earth at night to swim and play in the pool of the waterfall.

This graceful waterfall is one of three famous falls of Jeju—the others are Jeongbang, and Cheonjiyeon (the name of which, translated into English, is remarkably close the that of Cheonjeyeon; a fact that has been known to cause confusion with foreign visitors).

Far left: *The second impressive tier of the waterfall soars 98.5ft (30m) high. Around the falls, there are rare plants such as solipnan reeds, and the delicate Skeleton Fork fern.*

Top right: *Like so many waterfalls, the force of the flow varies according to the rainfall; it frequently falls in fine, graceful sheets, while at other times gushes with distinctive torrents caused by the projecting rocks at the lip.*

Right: *The first drop is 72ft (22m) high, plunging into a 69ft (21m) deep pool, the water coursing on toward the second tier across large boulders, the high banks overgrown with lush green trees and shrubs. Beyond the first tier an octagonal pavilion features a painting telling the legend of the nymphs.*

Seogwipo City, South Korea

SOUTH KOREA

Cheyonjeon Waterfall, Seogwipo City

- Jeju City
JEJU
- Seogwipo City

BRIDGE OF THE SEVEN NYMPHS

Above the waterfall, the gorge is spanned by the graceful Seonimgyo Bridge, also known as "Chilseonyeogyo," or "Seven Nymphs Bridge," which symbolizes the legend.

Both sides of the distinctive red and white bridge are adorned with 65.6ft (20m) figures of the nymphs—each playing musical instruments. The footbridge, completed in 1984, spans 420ft (128m), is 13.2ft (4m) wide, and has 100 guard rails, and 34 stone lanterns, which are illuminated at night. It links the Cheonjeyeon Waterfall with the Jungmun Tourist Complex.

Staubbach Falls

Lauterbrunnen, Switzerland

- **The Staubbach Falls is one of the most outstanding formations of its kind in Switzerland, a country with no shortage of magnificent waterfalls.**
- **The name Staubbach means "spray steam" in German.**
- **The waterfall plunges an impressive 982ft (299m) from a hanging valley onto cliffs that line the picturesque Lütschine River.**

Hanging valleys are formed when glaciers erode a valley so deeply that they leave the smaller tributary valleys, which enter them from either side, ending high above the valley floor.

After the glaciers have withdrawn, the water coming out of the tributaries has a long plunge to join the main valley river.

Unless tectonic movement or another Ice Age intervenes, the waters of Staubbach will eventually wear a channel in the mountainside so that they can flow into the Lütschine River by the gentlest possible gradient.

But if that change is ever completed, it will not be for millions of years. In the meantime, Staubbach Falls is one of the unmistakable and unmissable landmarks in the Bernese Oberland.

The falls came to world attention in the 18th century, when writers and artists visited Switzerland in increasing numbers while making the Grand Tour—a traditional journey of discovery and self-discovery around Europe that was undertaken by rich young men who had reached the end of their formal education.

Staubbach Falls remains a major attraction today; it is within easy reach of Interlaken by road, and a few minutes' walk from the train station of Lauterbrunnen village.

Far left: *Viewed from the village of Lauterbrunnen, with its elegant spired church, Staubbach Falls gushes from the overhanging cliff and cascades down the rock face, seemingly emptying directly among the houses. In the distance is the snow-capped peak of the Jungfrau mountain.*

Top right: *A constant source of sound and a stunning visual display, Staubbach Falls enhances the picture-postcard village of Lauterbrunnen. Even at night the display continues, when the falls are illuminated.*

Right: *The picturesque village of Lauterbrunnen nestles at the bottom of one of the most beautiful glacial valleys in Europe, surrounded by breathtaking mountain scenery, and dominated by the majestic Staubbach Falls, shown here as its plume of water is caught by the wind, creating a veil of mist.*

Lauterbrunnen, Switzerland

Staubbach Falls, Lauterbrunnen · Zurich

· Bern

Thun ·

· Lausanne

· Geneva

SONG OF THE SPIRITS

One of the first foreigners to memorialize Staubbach Falls was the German author Johann Wolfgang von Goethe (1749–1832), whose visit to the falls in 1779 inspired him to write a poem about it entitled *Gesang der Geister über den Wassern* (Song of the Spirits over the Waters). Soon set to music by Franz Schubert and translated into several languages, the lyric brought the previously unfrequented spot onto the itineraries of visitors from numerous countries.

Manai-no-taki Falls

Miyazaki, Japan

- **The beautiful Manai-no-taki Falls pour into the Gokase River in the province of Miyazaki on Japan's southern island of Kyushu.**
- **A plunge waterfall, the falls are one of the most popular attractions of the breathtaking Takachiho Gorge, which draws many visitors each year.**
- **The falls are considered to be one of the finest hundred waterfalls in Japan.**

In the northwest of the Miyuzaki province, surrounded by the Kyushu Mountains, lies the Japanese town of Takachiho. Nearby is the Takachiho Gorge, a picturesque, V-shaped gash in the ancient basalt rocks through which flow the crystal clear waters of the Gokase River. Plunging into the river from the top of a sheer cliff are the Manai-no-taki Falls. This beautiful, 56ft (17m) high waterfall creates drifting clouds of spray as its waters mingle with those of the river below.

The steep-sided gorge was created by the river cutting its way down through ancient lava beds that had been left by an eruption of the nearby Mount Aso volcano in the far distant past. The result is a narrow cleft with precipitous, red-tinted cliffs that rise above the emerald green water.

A well-signposted trail along the top of the gorge provides stunning views of the falls and the fractured basalt columns that make up the cliffs. Between spring and summer, the trail is fringed with sumptuous mountain cherry blossoms and the flowers of Japanese azaleas and wisteria, while in the fall, the scene become a riot of red and yellow foliage. Bridges over the gorge allow it to be seen from all angles.

Far left: *One of the best ways of enjoying the spectacle of the Manai-no-taki Falls is to rent a rowboat and gently float along the river past the tumbling cascade. It makes for a unique experience, the drifting spray cooling the air, while sunlight glitters on the water. The water is so clear that shoals of fish swimming below the boat can be seen quite clearly.*

Top right: *One of the three elegant bridges that cross the ravine allows fabulous views of the river 56ft (17m) below, and the graceful waterfall that cascades into it.*

Right: *An unabashed romantic vision, viewed from the bridge, as little rowboats coast past the exuberant plunge of the Manai-no-taki waterfall, in crystal clear emerald waters.*

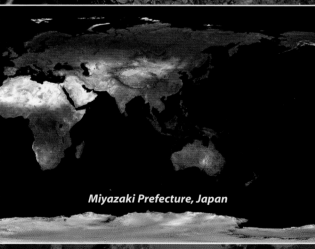

Miyazaki Prefecture, Japan

Fukuoka

• Beppu

• Kumamoto

Nagasaki •

KYUSHU

• *Miyazaki*

Manai-no-taki Falls, Miyazaki Prefecture

THE AMATERASU LEGEND

The area around the Takachiho Gorge is associated with many myths and legends concerning the founding of the Japanese nation. Close by is the Amano-Iwato Shrine, which marks the place where the sun goddess Amaterasu is said to have hidden in a cave because of her brother's cruelty. This plunged the world into endless night. Despite the pleas of the other gods, she would not emerge from the cave. Eventually, another goddess performed a suggestive dance that caused much mirth among the onlookers. Peering out of the cave to see what the uproar was about, Amaterasu was seized and pulled out to bring light to the world once more.

Havasu Falls

Havasupai Trail, Arizona, USA

• **Havasu Falls is a plunge fall that descends over a vertical cliff 120ft (37m) in height.**

• **It is located midway along the Havasupai Trail. This 8-mile (13km) path runs through parts of the Grand Canyon in Arizona and may be tackled without undue difficulty on foot or on a hired mule.**

• **The Trail begins at Hualapai Hilltop, 60 miles (96km) from Route 66, and extends to the small city of Supai.**

Havasu Falls is around halfway along the path from the highway, between two other interesting cascades—Navajo Falls and Mooney Falls. The main route runs over a wooden boardwalk right alongside the Havasu Falls; from there, a short detour leads onto a pathway through a small cavern behind the plunge.

Havasu Falls was named after the only indigenous inhabitants of the Grand Canyon, the Havasupai, a Native American people who have lived there for more than 800 years. There are now fewer than 1,000 of the Havasupai; most work in the local tourist industry, although some maintain the old traditional lifestyle, hunting in winter and farming in the summer months.

Havasu Falls is fed by Havasu Creek, a minor river that originates as snow and rain water around 50 miles (80km) away. From there the creek meanders across the plains before entering the Grand Canyon, where it receives further water from a thermal underground spring, which maintains a year-round temperature of 70°F (21°C). The creek then drops over the Havasu Falls, passes through Supai, and finally empties into the Colorado River.

Far left: *The sheer, natural beauty of Havasu Falls makes it one of the most photographed waterfalls in the world. The falls are in a constant sate of change, and sometimes the plunge separates into two separate chutes of water.*

Top right: *Viewed from above, the upper pool from which the plunge emanates can be seen, a vibrant blue-green much of the time, but often changing in hue due to the mineral deposits that are carried in the water. Swimming is permitted in the pools, and a rock shelter behind the plunge can also be reached. Although there are cliff jumping areas, jumping from the top of the falls is forbidden.*

Right: *The setting of Havasu Falls is like paradise on earth, beautiful, imposing and awe-inspiring in equal measures. Threatened by the destructive effects of flooding in the 1990s, which damaged the river above and below Havasu, and the falls themselves, a small dam was built above the plunge to preserve it for future generations to enjoy.*

Havasupai Tral, Arizona, USA

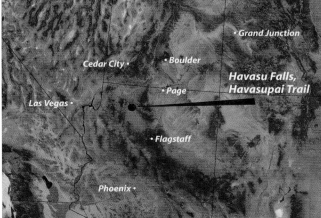

Grand Junction

Cedar City • Boulder

• Page

Havasu Falls, Havasupai Trail

Las Vegas •

• Flagstaff

Phoenix •

LIQUID KALEIDOSCOPE

Like much of the surrounding countryside, the bed of Havasu Creek is rich in minerals, and they are the cause of the frequent color changes in the waters. The predominant color is blue-green, which is derived from the abundant travertine deposits along its course. (A form of limestone, travertine is a dense, banded rock formed by the evaporation of spring waters and composed mainly of the mineral calcite.)

Yet because of the other minerals that drop into the Creek from time to time, the waters are often kaleidoscopic; people who are lucky enough to have seen them more than once attest that they never appear the same way twice.

Svartifoss

Skaftafell, Iceland

- **Although not the largest of Iceland's waterfalls, Svartifoss is instantly recognizable because of the color and unusual formation of the rocks that surround it.**

- **The falls are a major attraction of the Skaftafell National Park in southeastern Iceland, an area of outstanding natural beauty.**

- **This is a typical plunge waterfall, the water being thrown clear of the rock face in a narrow, graceful arc by the powerful force of the stream above.**

Iceland is known as a land of fire and ice. A combination of volcanic and glacial activity has produced, and continues to produce, a fascinating and naturally beautiful landscape, which is one of the major attractions for visitors to the country. In the southeast is the Skaftafell National Park, at 2,884 square miles (4,807sq km), the second largest of three national reserves and a region that is renowned for its pleasant climate. This reserve sits on one of the world's most extensive geothermal sites and includes Europe's largest glacier. The interplay between these two geological features has created some amazing natural wonders, which can easily be visited on foot thanks to an extensive network of hiking trails that runs throughout the park.

One of the most popular attractions in Skaftafell National Park is the Svartifoss, which means "Black Falls" in Icelandic. Located not far from the entrance to the park, the unusual type of heaxagonal rock formation that characterizes the falls can be found in lava flows that have cooled very slowly, leading to crystallization within the rock. Similar formations can be seen in Northern Ireland at the Giant's Causeway, and on the island of Staffa in Scotland.

Below the falls, the water crashes into a widening, crystal-clear plunge pool surrounded by the broken remnants of columns that have fallen from the cliff. Then it flows away downhill in a narrow stream that winds its way over and through a jumble of jagged rocks.

Far left: *The waterfall is named the "Black Falls" not for the color of the water, but rather for the color of the dark basalt rocks that make up the 39ft (12m) high, sheer cliff over which it plunges. These rocks take the form of hexagonal columns. In places, they have broken off, leaving the cliff face looking like a series of huge organ pipes.*

Top right: *At the base of the plunge are scattered many sharp chunks of rock that have broken away from the cliff above. Appearing unnaturally geometric in shape, these sections have broken off faster then the falling water is able to wear down their edges.*

Right: *During the coldest spell this curious natural phenomenon takes on a bizarre, other-worldly form, as the cascading water freezes, forming sharply pointed icicles that dangle from the hexagonal organ pipe columns of rock.*

ARCHITECTURAL INSPIRATION

The unusual formation of basalt columns that surround the Svartifoss has been an inspiration for some Icelandic architects. The "organ-pipe" shapes have been incorporated as decorative features in at least two major buildings in Reykjavik, the capital city of Iceland. One of them is an unusual-looking church called the Hallgrimskirkja, the other is the National Theater.

Skaftafell, Iceland

Svartifoss, Skaftafell

Húsavik

Budardalur

Reykjavik

Helmcken Falls

Wells Gray Provincial Park, British Columbia, Canada

- **With a straight plunge of 462ft (141m), Helmcken Falls is the fourth highest waterfall in Canada. It stands on the Murtle River in British Columbia.**
- **In addition to being one of the world's most beautiful and powerful waterfalls, it is one of the most recently discovered—it was first seen by Europeans in 1913.**
- **The attraction of Helmcken Falls was one of the main reasons for the designation of the surrounding land as an area of outstanding natural beauty, and the Canadian government decision to protect and nurture the region, which is now known as Wells Gray Provincial Park.**

Helmcken Falls is formed at the point where a great flat area of volcanic rock was worn away by waters released at the end of the last Ice Age to form a huge cliff—the geological term for this type of feature is a "fall line."

The falls are named for John Sebastian Helmcken (1824–1920), an English physician with the Hudson's Bay Company of fur traders that sought a northwest passage to the Pacific Ocean and did much to establish the British presence in Canada. Remarkably, Helmcken himself never saw the falls.

The falls are a plunge formation with a broad lip—around 300ft (100m) wide—that permits the passage of vast quantities of water at great speed: the amount per second is estimated at between 30,000 and 150,000 gallons (113,562–567,811 liters).

The Wells Gray Provincial Park authorities encourage the picturesque hike that leads to the top of the falls, while warning of the dangers of straying from the route. Although beautiful, the path takes visitors extremely close to the precipice. Numerous unfortunate people have fallen into the river and been swept to their deaths over the falls

Far left: *The best uninterrupted view of the falls can be attained by driving to the viewing platform. Alternatively, it is possible to take the 2–3 hour hike along the Helmcken Brink Trail, which follows the course of the Murtle River to the very top of the falls.*

Top right: *During winter Helmcken Falls freezes, and a huge volcano-like cone of ice forms at the base; its greatest recorded height is in excess of 200ft (60m).*

Right: *Thousands of gallons of water thunder over the broad lip of the falls and plummet into the chasm with an explosion of deafening noise and clouds of fine white spray.*

Wells Gray Provincial Park, Canada

Helmcken Falls, Wells Gray Provincial Park

Riske Creek

Kamloops •

Vancouver •

BEHIND THE FALLS

Behind the falls is a huge chamber, which has been eroded over millions of years by spray and ice. A footpath runs through the hollow enabling visitors to look out through the torrent at the outside world. This excursion is an unmissable part of any visit to Helmcken Falls—but beware, the noise of the water is deafening.

Natural Bridge

Numinbah Valley, Queensland, Australia

- **Also known as Natural Arch, this Australian waterfall lies in Numinbah Valley, Queensland, near the border with New South Wales, about a one-hour drive from Brisbane. It is a part of Springbrook National Park.**
- **The location takes its name from a basalt rock arch over Cave Creek, a small waterway near the source of the Nerang River.**
- **The falls themselves have retreated since the arch was formed, and now make a magnificent backdrop to this magical scene.**

The arch itself was formed by the waterfall when it eroded its own base until it opened up a preexistent underground cavern; having done that, its waters then worked their way back to the surface a short distance downstream. The two holes thus created formed a semicircle of rock above the water.

Natural Bridge is worthy of two visits—one by day, to appreciate the extraordinary structure, and another by night: the cave is home to a vast colony of glow worms that illuminate the darkness with thousands of tiny points of green light; meanwhile, the surrounding subtropical rainforest is lit by luminous fungi and a host of fireflies.

Swimming is permitted in the cave, although diving into the pool is forbidden on safety grounds.

A path from the splash pool leads round to the top of the falls, where the lush vegetation features a range of fruit trees in which brush-tailed possums are often seen.

The Natural Bridge is part of the ancestral territory of the Kombumerri aboriginal people.

Far left: *Natural Bridge is an enchanting grotto, where water plunges uninterrupted through an opening in its roof. The feature as created when the waterfall undercut a cave beneath it, and dug a pothole on top, until the two joined and the creek began to flow through the cave.*

Top right: *Visitors are permitted to swim in the cave, and enjoy a nocturnal tour to see the glow worms which inhabit the cave. On summer nights luminous fungi and fireflies create an ethereal display. On warm summer evenings it is possible to hear the calls of paradise riflebirds, green catbirds, and wompoo fruit-doves.*

Right: *Resembling the gateway to a magical kingdom, the entrance to the cave was created as the water, collected within, sought an exit. Inside this curious structure, the waterfall pours gently from a hole near the center of the cave.*

Queensland, Australia

Toowoomba •   Brisbane •

Nerang •

Warwick •   • Tweed Heads

Balina •

Natural Bridge, Queensland

SEASONAL VISITS

Although the Natural Bridge receives most visitors during the summer (December–March), this is the wettest time of year: the park receives an average of 59in (150cm) of rain during this period. Winters there are drier, but because of Springbrook's altitude—3,000ft (900m) above sea level—they can be surprisingly cool.

Gaping Gill

Ingleborough, North Yorkshire Dales, England

- **Gaping Gill (alternatively Gaping Ghyll) is the highest unbroken waterfall in England.**
- **The falls drops from the surface of the North Yorkshire Dales near Ingleborough, the second highest peak in the region, into a cavern 360ft (110m) beneath the earth.**
- **Potholers can make the trip underground between Gaping Gill and Ingleborough Cave—their average journey time from end to end is 16 hours.**

Fell Beck, the stream that passes through Gaping Ghyll, resurfaces after a few miles near the village of Clapham, where it flows out of Ingleborough Cave, a magnificent structure that contains an array of unusually shaped stalagmites and stalactites. Some of these calcium carbonate deposits—such as The Jockey's Cap and The Elephant—are named after what they appear to resemble.

The whole area around this amazing geological feature is a limestone plateau that effectively forms the roof of an extensive network of caves that descend to depths of up to 600ft (183m).

There are several points of access to this subterranean nether world, although the two main entrances are at White Scar Cave and Skirwith Cave, both of which are open to the general public. Potholers can enter through a host of other adits (horizontal drainage passages), known as "pots," including the quirkily named Corky's Pot, Disappointment Pot, and Flood Entrance Pot.

The first human known to have successfully reached the bottom of Gaping Gill was the French speleologist Édouard-Alfred Martel (1859–1938), who achieved his feat in 1895.

Far left: *Perhaps one of the most unusual and somewhat sinister locations for a waterfall, the underground cavern into which the Gaping Gill waterfall plunges is an awe-inspiring sight for those who dare enter.*

Top right: *From the surface, Gaping Gill is an awesome sight—a vast hole in the earth, into which the waters of Fell Beck gush in the form of a spectacular waterfall that can only be seen from the subterranean world.*

Right: *The sight of Fell Beck plunging twice the height of Niagara Falls into a dark, foreboding abyss is nothing short of spectacular. Here an adventurous visitor is lowered in a special harness through the waterfall itself, during one of the popular "Winch Weekend" meetings.*

North Yorkshire Dales, England

Gaping Gill, Ingleborough

• Carlisle

• Bridlington

• Harrogate

Morcambe •

• Liverpool

INTO THE ABYSS

During peak holiday periods, members the Bradford Pothole Club and the Craven Pothole Club offer members of the public giddy rides by rope winch to the bottom of Gaping Gill, during "Winch Weekend." Fortuitously, return tickets only are sold.

Jeongbang Waterfall

Seogwipo City, South Korea

- **Jeongbang is one of the most famous waterfalls on Jeju Island, off the southern coast of South Korea.**
- **It is a plunge formation with a drop of 75ft (23m).**
- **Jeju was formed by eruptions of Mount Halla, a now extinct volcano that rises to 6,398ft (1,950m) at the center of the island.**

The Jeongbang Waterfall was formed around 10,000 years ago at the end of the last Ice Age by fresh water seeking the shortest route to the sea over hard volcanic rock through which it has not yet had time to erode a gentle, sloping course.

Jeongbang is often described as the only waterfall in Asia that falls directly into the sea. That assertion is contentious, because it actually lands in a small, sheltered cove, but many guidebooks omit to point that out, and indeed in layman's terms it may be a distinction completely without a difference.

There is an observatory near the top of the falls with a fine view of the sea; refreshments are sold and there are also recreational facilities. To the east of the Jeongbang Waterfall, and a little way inland, is another waterfall, Sojeongbang, which, though smaller and slightly less impressive, is well worth the walk of only around 300 yd (275m).

Jeju is known as Korea's "honeymoon island," since it attracts a large number of domestic tourists form in and around Korea.

Far left: *The picturesque Jeongbang Waterfall plunges from a high cliff overlooking the sea, then filters from its plunge pool across a small cove strewn with large boulders.*

Top right: *The twin plunges of the fall cascade onto the large pile of stones that litter the base of the drop, immediately before the plunge pool. The force of the water sends spray and mist dancing in the air.*

Right: *Emerging from the lip of the fall, the two main plunges descend 75ft (23m) to the base, cascading onto the rocks. The fact that the water does not discharge directly into the sea does not detract from the falls' overriding charm.*

Seogwipo City, South Korea

SOUTH KOREA

Jeongbang Waterfall, Seogwipo City

Jeju City
JEJU
Seogwipo City

SEARCH FOR ETERNAL YOUTH

According to legend, an ancient Chinese emperor of the great conquering Qin dynasty (221–207 BC) heard that on the slopes of Mount Halla grew a herb that gave the user eternal youth. He sent his servant, Seo Bul, to look for it. Although his search ended in failure, Seo Bul was so enchanted by the beauty of Jeongbang that he inscribed "Seobulgwacha" on the cliff face beside it, which means "Seo Bul passed this place." The action of the water have since erased his autograph, although a modern replica now features.

Maletsunyane Falls

Semonkong, Lesotho, Southern Africa

• **Maletsunyane Falls is also known as Semonkong Falls or Le Bihan Falls, after a 19th-century French missionary who visited the site.**

• **The falls have a drop of 630ft (192m), making them Africa's highest plunge formation and the continent's fourth highest waterfall of any kind.**

• **They stand at the point where the Maletsunyane River reaches the edge of a basalt plateau that adjoins a sandstone depression.**

Maletsunyane Falls is around 3 miles (5km) from Semonkong, a small town whose name—meaning "Place of Smoke"—refers to the mists created by the tumbling waters. The easy walk from the lodge to the waterfall passes through an amazing variety of flora, including fields of flowering lilies; bearded vultures may often be seen circling overhead.

The town is interesting in itself, receiving its electric power from the river, via a miniature hydroelectric plant. It hosts a monthly horse race, in addition to trading in horses, wool, and farm produce.

Maletsunyane Falls is at its most spectacular in the summer (December-March), when the flow is at its strongest, but is well worth a visit during the winter months (June-August), when unwary travelers may be surprised to find that the falls are frozen, and the plunge pool has turned into a great dome of ice. These extremes of climate are produced by Lesotho's topography: the country is landlocked and mountainous, with an average elevation of around 8,000ft (2,500m) above sea level. During warmer weather, the plunge pool at the base of Maletsunyane Falls is safe and suitable for swimming.

On the trek to the falls it is not uncommon to encounter bands of nomadic horsemen dressed in colorful blankets, carrying rifles, while barefooted locals may appear to offer to guide the visitor to the falls, and the plunge pool at the base.

Far left: *An arresting, remote scene amid rolling terrain, Maletsunyane Falls is distinctive for its single plunge into a gorge with steep, rugged walls.*

Top right: *The trip down into the base of the gorge is a strenuous one hour hike along a difficult path, and the return journey taxing, although the sense of achievement visitors feel is considerable.*

Right: *The water spray at the base of the falls is so intense that clothes will be drenched within minutes, and cameras rendered useless—but the effort in reaching the plunge pool is always well worth it, when the weather permits a cooling swim.*

THE QUICK DESCENT

Walking down into the base of the falls is just not exciting enough for some people, who prefer a more exhilarating method. The sheer rock face beside the Maletsunyane Falls has been authenticated by the *Guinness Book of Records* as the site of the world's longest single-drop abseil, and many adventurers take the opportunity to descend by this extreme method. Despite this quick way down, however, the long hike back up is still obligatory.

Semonkong, Lesotho, Southern Africa

• Bloemfontein

• Maseru

LESOTHO

Durban •

SOUTH AFRICA

Maletsunyane Falls, Semonkong

Yosemite Falls

Yosemite National Park, California, USA

Far left: *The Upper Falls is formed by the swift waters of Yosemite Creek, which, after meandering through Eagle Creek Meadow, hurl themselves over the edge of a hanging valley in a spectacular and deafening show of force.*

- **Yosemite falls is the highest measured waterfall in North America.**
- **The 2,425ft (739m) distance from the top of the upper falls to the base of the lower falls qualifies Yosemite Falls as the sixth highest waterfall in the world.**
- **The maximum recorded volume for Yosemite falls is 12,716 gallons (48,138 liters) per second.**

Yosemite falls is located in Yosemite National Park in the Sierra Nevada mountains of California. It is a major attraction in the park, especially in late spring when the water flow is at its peak. Although often referred to as a "two-stage drop," the falls actually consist of three sections: the 1,430ft (425m) plunge qualifies the Upper Falls alone as one of the twenty highest waterfalls in the world. Trails up from the valley floor and down from other regions of the park outside the valley proper lead to both the top and base of Upper Yosemite Falls.

Between the two obvious main plunges there is a series of cascades and smaller plunges generally referred to as "the cascades." Taken together these account for another drop of 675ft (205m), more than twice the height of the Lower Falls. Because of the layout of the area, the lack of any major drops in this section, and the lack of public access, they are often overlooked. Several vantage points for the cascades are found along the Yosemite Falls trail. The final 320ft (97m) drop of the Lower Falls, adjacent to an accessible viewing area, provides the most-used viewing point for the waterfalls.

Yosemite Creek emerges from the base of the Lower Falls and flows into the Merced River nearby. Like many areas of Yosemite the plunge pool at the base of the Lower Falls is surrounded by dangerous jumbles of talus made even more treacherous by the high humidity and resulting slippery surfaces. In years of little snow, the falls may actually cease flowing altogether in late summer or fall.

Top right: *The top of the Upper Falls can be reached after a demanding steep 3.5-mile (5.6km) hike from the Sunnyside campground, or via numerous routes to the north of the falls, from the Tioga Road.*

Right: *The falls viewed from the floor of the Yosemite Valley are an astonishingly beautiful sight, as the white plume of the Upper Falls crashes down the sheer face amid clouds of spray, its waters emerging in the Lower Falls, from where they empty into the Merced River.*

Yosemite National Park, California, USA

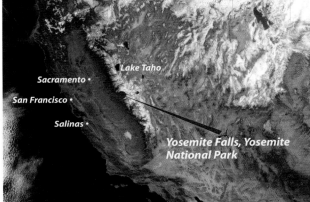

Sacramento
Lake Taho
San Francisco
Salinas
Yosemite Falls, Yosemite National Park

THE AHWAHNEECHEE LEGEND

The Ahwahneechee people of Yosemite Valley called the waterfall "Cholock" and believed that the plunge pool at its base was inhabited by the spirits of several witches, called the Poloti. An Ahwaneechee folktale describes a woman going to fetch a pail of water from the pool, and drawing it out full of snakes. Later that night, after the woman had trespassed into their territory, the spirits caused the woman's house to be sucked into the pool by a powerful wind, taking the woman and her newborn baby with her. It is thought that the story was made-up to caution people from approaching the dangerous splash pool.

Angel Falls

Bolivar state, Venezuela

- **At a height of 3,212ft (979m), Salto Angel, or "Angel Falls" is the world's highest waterfall. The local Pemon people named the falls Kerepakupai Merú, which means "fall from the deepest place."**
- **The first 2,648ft (807m) is a freefalling plunge, the longest in the world, with the water often turned to mist by the high winds before reaching the bottom.**
- **The falls are situated in Canaima National Park, a large reserve that borders Brazil and Guyana, and is a UNESCO World Heritage Site.**

Canaima National Park is famed for the spectacular *tepuis*—flat table mountains of fractured sandstone with sheer sides—that are of great geological interest. The source of the water above Angel Falls is rainfall—up to 300in (762cm) of rainfall collects in ravines, cracks, and crevasses at the top of Auyán Tepuí ("Devils Mountain"), and pours out of the sheer cliff face, touching rock only when it reaches the bottom. The water then slides down a steep area of sloping rock to form a cascade fall of 100ft (30.4m). The falls averages 350ft (107m) in width, with the base measuring 500ft (150m). The water feeds into the Rio Gauja.

Canaima National Park hosts an amazing variety of flora and fauna, including poison arrow frogs and hundreds of species of orchids. Those hardy enough to tackle the trek to the falls may spot monkeys, giant anteaters, armadillos, three-toed sloths, jaguars, tapirs and capybaras.

There are two ways to reach the falls: by boat or by plane. The journey by boat can take up to four days, though there is a shorter voyage by motorboat that will also involve an arduous trek through the rainforest to reach the base of the falls. During the dry season (January–April), the low level of the river makes the journey even more difficult, if not impossible. In addition, the falls can be reduced to a trickle during this period, with the water vaporizing into mist before reaching the base. The rainy season, when the falls are at full strength, runs from June to October. The expedition by a light aircraft is considerably less arduous, and probably provides the most spectacular views, as the aircraft flies over and in front of the falls.

Left: *The view of Angel Falls from the base is astonishing, as water cascades from the top of the table mountain. From here the water feeds into the Rio Guaja, which then flows into the Churun River, a tributary of the Carrao River.*

Top right: *A spectacular view of Angel Falls from Ilsa Ratón ("Mouse Island", in the Orinoco River, where many visitors spend the night before trekking to the base of the falls. The hike takes around one hour from this point, passing through lush jungle.*

Right: *The falls are Venezuela's main tourist attraction, but reaching them is arduous. Even on arrival, there is no guarantee that you will actually see this great natural wonder—it can remain tantalizingly concealed on cloudy days, while the mist formed by the plunging water itself can obscure the view.*

Venezuela, South America

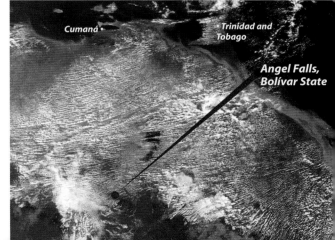

Cumaná · *Trinidad and Tobago*

Angel Falls, Bolívar State

JIMMY ANGEL

Though he was not the first to discover the falls, the American pilot Jimmy Angel was the first to bring the wonder to the world's attention. Seeking his fortune in gold, Angel was scouring the rainforest when he spotted the falls in 1933. He returned four years later with his wife and two explorers, and attempted to land his monoplane on top of the flat tepui. The plane promptly sank into a bog. Angel and his party had to walk back to camp though the inhospitable terrain, arriving exhausted and starving 11 days later. A legend was born. The plane stayed at the top of the tepui for 33 years, and is now at the Aviation Museum in Maracay. A replica has been placed back on top of the tepui.

Palouse Falls

Palouse State Park, Washington, USA

- **Palouse Falls lies on the Palouse River in Washington State, around 4 miles (6km) above its confluence with the Snake River.**
- **This formation, which comprises a plunge, a cascade, and a fan, has a total drop of 183ft (56m) from the top to the deep green pool at the bottom.**
- **The whole region in which the Palouse Falls is located is something of a geological anomaly—a desert that can simultaneously sustain both rivers and waterfalls.**

The explanation for the geological formation is that, during the Ice Age, the ice barrier that contained what is now Lake Missoula periodically broke, releasing vast quantities of water that have shaped the amazing modern topography.

There is a footpath down the side of the Palouse Falls, but walkers take it at their own risk: Palouse State Park rangers stress that they will not be responsible for their safety because of the risks that are posed by avalanches and rattlesnakes.

Below the falls, the Palouse River enters a series of five rapids, which are quite undemanding to paddle down but very hard to reach: the only way is by hauling the boats upstream.

There are 10 campsites within easy reach of the falls, but none is well developed, a fact that is both a cause and an effect of the very small number of visitors to the area.

In prehistoric times, the Palouse River flowed into the Columbia River, but great floods during the Pleistocene Epoch, between 1.6 million and 10,000 years ago, raised the level of the water above the southern lip of the canyon and enabled it to redirect itself to the Snake River. Its former course can still be seen: it is now a dry arroyo (steep-sided gully), the Washtucna Coulee.

Far left: *A forbidding landscape of sheer basalt canyon walls that rise 377ft (115m) above the riverbanks surround the Palouse Falls. At the very top, left of picture, generations of wind erosion has carved serrated edges to the rocks that resemble the battlements of a castle.*

Top right: *From the vantage point on the opposite cliff, the delicate beauty of the water as it cascades from the ledge may help to soften the overall ruggedness of the terrain, but the falls are themselves a powerful and primeval force to be reckoned with.*

Right: *The Palouse Waterfall sits at the center of a rock-rimmed aphitheater, the water plunging into an intensely green pool, the sides of the cliff clothed with green algae.*

GIANT TALE

According to a legend of the indigenous Palouse Indians, the Palouse River flowed smoothly until four giant brothers caught a giant beaver. Each of the hunters speared the creature once, and every time it was wounded it scrabbled with its paws at the walls of the canyon, eventually gouging a hole through which the river then flowed until it came to a cliff edge, the site of the falls. When stripped of its mythological trappings, this story may suggest that the redirection of the river took place within human memory.

Palouse State Park, Washington, USA

Vancouver

Seattle

Spokane

Moses Lake

Kennewick

Palouse Falls, Palouse State Park

Vøringsfossen

Eidfjord, Hordaland, Norway

- **Around 6 miles (10km) from the end of Eidfjord, a finger of deep water that extends south from the vast Hardangerfjord, Vøringsfossen is the most famous waterfall in Norway.**

- **Thanks to its convenient location, close to the main road between Bergen, 93 miles (150km) to the west, and Oslo, 185 miles (300km) to the south, it is also one of the most visited.**

- **The main cascade drops 535ft (163m) from the sub-Arctic tundra of the Hardangevidda into the heart of a great nature center at its foot.**

Vøringsfossen was formed at the end of the last Ice Age, when the polar icecap withdrew during a prehistoric period of global warming to reveal the modern topography of Scandinavia.

For the next 10,000 years, this wonder of nature remained largely undiscovered. Even as late as the 18th century, the only people who really knew about it were a few locals.

That began to change after a Norwegian professor named Christopher Hansteen crossed Hardangervidda in the summer of 1821 to make astronomical observations.

In the course of his journey he came across several spectacular waterfalls, but when a man he met on the path offered to show him a cascade that was 4,500ft (1,400m) high, he followed him only because he did not believe such a thing possible.

Hansteen was right in that assumption, but what he did see was in no way disappointing. He attempted to calculate the true height of Vøringsfossen using the only appropriate instrument at his disposal—a stone, which he dropped over the edge and counted the seconds until it landed. The result he produced—933ft (280m)—was almost twice the actual figure, but his written account of Vøringsfossen accurately described the beauty of the falls and brought them to international attention.

The subsequent construction of the trunk road brought these magnificent falls within reach.

Far left: *From one of the viewpoints at the head of the falls, numerous courses converge and plummet downward into the Måbø Valley, and then create a river that winds it way through the valley floor. Another viewpoint is located—apparently rather precariously—where a virtual head-on aspect of the falls can be witnessed, top left of picture.*

Top right: *A trail from the top of the falls leads down to the bottom, where the adventurous visitor can relish another fine perspective of this natural wonder—and there are likely to be fewer people to interrupt the view than at the top.*

Right: *The main cascade gushes down the rock face, creating clouds of spray as it hits the plunge pool at the base, which then pours down the fast flowing watercourse and through the Hardangevidda Nature Center.*

Eidfjord, Hordaland, Norway

Vøringsfossen, Eidfjord

Bergen

Stavanger

Oslo

Fredrikstad

WATERFALL ON TAP

One of the most remarkable features of Vøringsfossen is that its waters are human-controlled and turned on and off like a faucet. Every year, on September 15, the authorities declare the tourist season at a close and redirect the flow to a nearby hydroelectric power plant. At the beginning of spring, they allow the torrent to return to its natural course.

Calf Creek Falls

Calf Creek Recreation Area, Utah, USA

- There are two desert waterfalls along Calf Creek. The more famous Lower Calf Creek Falls are 126ft (38m) high. The upper falls, 2.5 miles (4km) upstream, are 88ft (27m) high.

- Calf Creek Canyon paints a stroke of greenery through the surrounding landscape of distinctive cream-colored Navajo sandstone.

- Passing between mineral-streaked cliffs, hikers pass beaver ponds and prehistoric rock art sites on their way to the falls.

The sandy access track, to Lower Calf Creek Falls is 2.7 miles (4.4km) long, and at first skirts the side of the canyon and then descends onto the canyon floor, passing clear, deep ponds and marshes. The falls are hidden from view until visitors round a corner at the end of the walking track, but clearly audible before that.

The falls, and the creek itself, take their name from the practice of the early settlers, who would turn out weaned calves, just taken from their mothers, into the natural pasture within the box canyon.

The water in the valley, including the perennial Calf Creek itself, feeds cottonwood trees and Utah junipers. The path to the upper falls is slightly more difficult, leading from the main highway down a steep slope of slick rock, but there are cairns of volcanic pebbles to mark the way.

Calf Creek is a tributary of the slow, shallow Escalante River, which flows into Lake Powell. They are all part of the Grand Staircase-Escalante National Monument, a 1.7 million-acre (688,000ha) geological spectacle of cliffs, plateaus, canyons, sandstone arches, natural bridges, monoliths, and balanced rocks.

The Escalante Canyons form a maze created by the river and its tributaries, much of which has still not been thoroughly explored.

Far left: *Because the waterfall faces southeast, the area around the plunge pool is in shade for most of the day, creating a cool, misty haven, with a beach and even volcanic boulders people can launch off into the pool.*

Top right: *The roaring water of the Lower Calf Creek Falls emerges from V-shaped channel, plunging onto a rock ledge, plunging again, then cascading over rocks that are carpeted with blue-green algae.*

Right: *The sculptural quality of the rock face through which the water gushes is typical of the area. The distinctive water markings that streak the rocks are known as "desert varnish."*

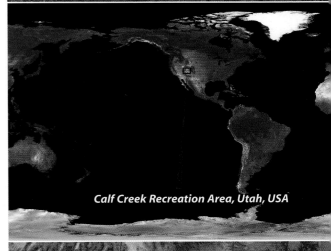

Calf Creek Recreation Area, Utah, USA

Calf Creek Falls, Calf Creek Recreation Area

NATIVE AMERICAN PAST

En route to Calf Creek Falls there is ample evidence of inhabitation, between 800 and 1,000 years ago, of the Native American Anasazi and Fremont cultures. The remains of two grain stores are tucked in rock alcoves, and a rock painting depicts four large figures in red. The area is also a plentiful source of fossils. The Escalante River is thought to be the last major river to be discovered on the US mainland, and the nearby town of Boulder was the last to receive its post by mule trains. Isolation and inhospitable terrain have probably helped to protect many local sites of historical interest. This unique topography does not allow ready public access.

Montmorency Falls

Quebec, Canada

• **The Montmorency Falls is a major tourist attraction outside the city of Quebec in Canada.**

• **The large block waterfall is the tallest in the province of Quebec and, at 275ft (84m), is 98ft (30m) higher than Niagara Falls.**

• **The falls were the site of an unsuccessful attempt by British troops under General Wolfe to seize Quebec from the French in 1759.**

The Montmorency Falls is a dramatic waterfall that is located in a park about 6 miles (10km) to the east of the city of Quebec. The waters crash down a near-vertical cliff at the mouth of the Montmorency River, where it enters the St. Lawrence River, opposite the western end of the Ile d'Orleans. At the foot of the falls is a 56ft (17m) deep, bowl-shaped plunge pool. The water often has a yellow cast caused by the high iron content of the riverbed.

The falls were discovered in 1613 by the renowned French explorer Samuel de Champlain, who traveled extensively throughout much of the area and was instrumental in opening up North America to the fur trade. He also founded the city of Quebec and was popularly known as the "father of New France," the French colony established in the eastern region of what would eventually become Canada. Champlain named the river and falls in honor of Henri II, Duke of Montmorency, the governor of Languedoc and an admiral of the French navy, who subsequently served as viceroy of New France between 1620 and 1625.

A suspension bridge spanning the river offers spectacular views of the falls. An earlier version of the bridge collapsed about a hundred years ago, sending three people to their deaths, but the present example is totally safe.

There are also trails through the park that lead to scenic overlooks that provide impressive views of the falls.

Far left: *Quebec city's proud boast is that Montmorency Falls is 98ft (30m) taller than the famous Niagara Falls, although is is far narrower. Nevertheless, the falls is a grand spectacle close to the city, and the environs have been sensitively developed in order that visitors can experience the power and beauty of this natural wonder.*

Top right: *A variety of means have been provided so that visitors can enjoy the beauty of the falls to the full. For the energetic, there is a set of 487 stairs, interspersed with observation decks, that snake their way up the cliff face to the top. Alternatively, it is possible to ride a cablecar to the top, where a suspension bridge spans the crest of the falls, providing a unique view of the cascade.*

Right: *The falls are illuminated at night, casting an eerie glow, particularly in winter when the waters often partially freeze. During the summer, two nights a week from late July to mid-August, the falls act as a backdrop to a spectacular international fireworks competition, Le Grands Feux Loto-Québec.*

Quebec, Canada

Baie-Comeau •

Lake St-Jean
• Alma

• Rimouski

Baie-St-Paul •

Montmorency Falls, Quebec

Quebec •

A MILITARY PAST

The park surrounding the Montmorency Falls contains the remnants of earthworks that were constructed by British soldiers in 1759 during the Battle of Quebec, when Britain was attempting to seize control of French territory in North America. In an attempt to defeat the French forces under General Montcalm, who held Quebec, the British General Wolfe landed troops at the foot of the falls, where they attempted to attack by climbing the cliffs, but poor discipline led to them being repulsed with a loss of 440 men. Subsequently, Wolfe's men launched a surprise attack by scaling cliffs below the Plains of Abraham and captured the city.

Gullfoss

Hvítá, Southern Iceland

• **Gullfoss ("Golden Falls") is the most famous waterfall in Iceland. It stands on the Hvítá River.**

• **The Hvítá River is a tributary of the Ölfusá, which is fed by meltwaters from the Lang Glacier, located in the center of the country.**

• **On sunlit days the mist clouds created by the falls are filled with dozens of rainbows in a wonderful spectacle of color and motion.**

About half a mile (1km) above the falls, the Hvítá River ("White River") turns abruptly to its left and then tumbles down in two initial stages—the first 36ft (11m) high, the second 69ft (21m) high—into a deep crevice, the Gullfossgjúfur, around 1.5 miles (2.5km) long and only 60ft (20m) wide.

Geologists believe that the crevice, or canyon, was formed during torrential flooding, caused by the jökulhlaup (glacial outbursts), that occurred near the end of the ice age.

Gullfoss is deafeningly powerful. The average volume of water that flows through it is between 30,800 gallons (116,590 liters) per second in summer and 17,600 gallons (66,623 liters) per second in winter. The highest throughput ever recorded is 440,000 gallons (1.7 million liters) per second.

For much of the 20th century, there was considerable political pressure to harness this great natural resource by constructing a dam and a hydroelectric power plant, a project that would have changed the character of the falls. However, owing to a combination of logistical difficulties and opposition from environmentalists, nothing ever happened, and Gullfosss is now protected against development.

Far left: *One of the most unusual features of Gullfoss is the fact that its main step—a drop of 105ft (32m)—is at a right angle to the flow of the river. The next step plunges into a deep narrow crevice. On approaching the falls the crevice is not visible, so it appears that the entire river simply disappears into the earth.*

Top right: *The 230ft (70m) deep crevice, viewed along its length, channels the entire broad river into a width of no more than 60ft (20m), and runs for 1.5 miles (2.5km).*

Right: *Visitors can admire the falls from two main viewpoints, one close to the edge of the first, broad drop, the other from the high cliff further upstream (far left of picture).*

Hvítá, Iceland

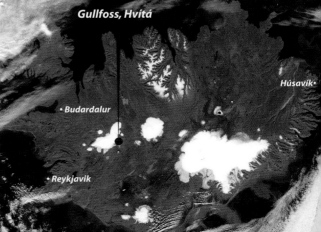

Gullfoss, Hvítá

Húsavík•

• Budardalur

• Reykjavik

GOLDEN CIRCLE

Gullfoss is one of the most popular tourist destinations in Iceland. It is within easy reach of the capital, Reykjavik, and forms one of the main stops on the so-called "Golden Circle" tour, a day trip that also takes in the hot springs at Geysir (the place that gave its name to the phenomenon), and Thingvellir, the site of the original Icelandic open-air Althing (parliament), and the point at which the European and American tectonic plates are separating.

Rhine Falls

Schaffhausen, Switzerland

- **The Rhine Falls is located 2 miles (3km) southwest of the city of Schaffhausen in northern Switzerland, close to the German border.**
- **It is a cataract formation which is split into two sections by a huge rock pillar in midstream.**
- **Known in German as Der Rheinfall, this is generally accepted as being the most spectacular waterfall in central Europe.**

Rhine Falls is so widely regarded not so much for its height, a comparatively modest 75ft (23m), nor even for its width, an impressive but by no means overwhelming 450ft (150m), but for its sheer power.

In the winter months, when the flow is at its lowest because the river's sources in the Alps are frozen, the falls are traversed by 55,000 gallons (208,198 liters) per second; in summer, when the peaks are melting, that figure rises to 132,000 gallons (500,000 liters) per second.

As their name suggests, the falls stand on the Rhine, one of the longest, biggest, and most important rivers in Europe, which flows for 865 miles (1,390km) from its source in the Swiss Alps to its mouth on the North Sea. They were formed in the latter part of the last Ice Age, between around 17,000 and 14,000 years ago.

The falls leave a lasting impression with anyone who encounters it. The famous German Romantic poet Eduard Mörike once wrote: "Oh, traveler, be careful and hold your heart very firm in your hands—I nearly lost mine out of joy by watching the powerful play of huge masses of water thundering down the falls and breaking the surface below, causing a mist rising high..."

Far left: *The ultimate way to experience the might of the broad river as t surges over these magnificent falls is to take a boat trip to the central rock.*

Top right: *A fle of brave tourists clambers up the steep stone staircase that leads to the top of the Rhine Falls' central rock, which proudly displays the Swiss flag at its peak. The sheer power of the water is evident as it crashes in a mass of white spray against the somewhat flimsy looking rock.*

Right: *A pleasure boat cruises close to the mighty torrent pouring from the fall, enveloped in spray. In the background is an arched railway bridge with pedestrian access, which crosses the Rhine. On a promontory beside the river, the whole scene is dominated by the Schloss Laufen, a medieval turreted castle, from where a path leads down to a "Känzeli," or lookout cantilevered over the water.*

Schaffhausen, Switzerland

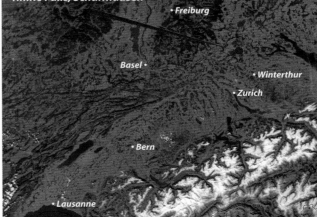

Rhine Falls, Schaffhausen

- Freiburg
- Basel
- Winterthur
- Zurich
- Bern
- Lausanne

UP CLOSE

The Rhine Falls is a major tourist attraction, and pleasure boats sail out regularly from the banks to the middle of the river, where the power of the water rattles the hulls and the noise makes normal speech incredibly difficult.

Some trips land at the base of the central rock, from which a rock stairway leads to the summit.

Kaieteur Falls

Kaieteur National Park, Guyana

• **This block waterfall in central Guyana is 741ft (226m) high, five times higher than the Niagara Falls and only 9ft (3m) shorter than the Tower of the Americas in San Antonio, Texas.**

• **It stands on the Potaro River, which during the rainy season is more than 400ft (122m) wide at its point of entry into the main drop.**

• **With an average of 146,000 gallons (552,700 liters) flowing over it every second, it is among the 20 most powerful waterfalls in the world.**

Guyana is the only nation state of the Commonwealth of Nations on the mainland of South America. Kaieteur Falls is the main attraction in the Kaieteur National Park, a protected rainforest that is a popular excursion destination from Guyana's capital, Georgetown.

Most tourists fly to the area by chartered aircraft, landing on a nearby airstrip surrounded by jungle; the falls are a 1 mile (1.6km) hike through the jungle from the airstrip. Overland journeys to the falls are also possible, commonly involving a three to five days excursion.

The falls currently attract only around 2,000 foreign visitors a year. The surrounding area is correspondingly unspoiled, especially at the top of the falls, where there is thick tropical vegetation; swifts soar overhead and tapirs, monkeys, and anteaters may be seen in the undergrowth.

Downstream from the main plunge—which occurs as the water reaches the edge of the Pakaraima Plateau, a sandstone rock formation—the falls have carved out a vast gorge, 5 miles (8km) long, that takes the Potaro down another 81ft (25m) over a series of cascades.

Far left: *Kaieteur Falls are in a remote, unspoilt location with no signs of civilization. There are no safety features such as railings at the edge of the basin into which the waters plunge, other than polite notices which read "Please keep 8ft away from the edge of the cliff." Few visitors, however, obey this rule in order to peer over the precipice or have their photograph taken with the magnificent cascade behind them.*

Top right: *It is easy to see how the majesty and sheer power of the falls has made a lasting impression on the landscape and the people of the region. They are a fascinating and important link to the past. According to one local legend, the falls were named for Kai, a prehistoric Amerindian chief, who, it is said, paddled over the edge to save his people by sacrificing himself to the gods.*

Right: *In the rainy season the volume of water passing over the falls is prodigious, gushing into the gorge, where clouds of whispy steam erupt and rainbows are frequently formed in the humid atmosphere.*

DANGEROUS SWIM

The first European to set eyes on Kaieteur Falls was Charles Barrington Brown, one of a team of British geologists who surveyed the region in 1870. In 1955, another Briton, the soldier Robert Howat swam across the top of the Kaieteur Falls. He was almost pulled over the lip, but managed to cling onto some weeds around 30ft (10m) from the drop until he was pulled to safety by a local man.

Howat's feat was logged in the 1970 edition of the *Guinness Book of Records* as the most dangerous swim on record, but 10 years later he persuaded the publishers to remove it in case anyone else attempted to emulate him.

Kaieteur National Park, Guyana

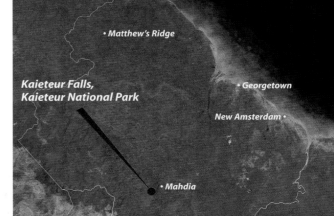

• Matthew's Ridge

Kaieteur Falls,
Kaieteur National Park

• Georgetown

New Amsterdam •

• Mahdia

Dettifoss

Mývatn, Iceland

- **Dettifoss is considered to be one of the most powerful waterfalls in Europe, with an estimated 110,000 gallons (500,000 liters) pouring over the falls every second, depending on the season.**
- **The fall has a drop of 144ft (44m), and has an average width of 328ft (100m).**
- **The waterfall lies along Iceland's second longest river, Jökulsá á Fjöllum.**

Dettifoss is fed by the ice melt that travels down the Jökulsá á Fjöllum River from the Vatnajökull glacier. The canyon below the falls is Jökulsárgljúfur, now part of a national park.

The canyon was formed 8,000 years ago, when a volcano erupted under the river, causing catastrophic explosions that blew apart the mountains. The result was an extraordinary landscape, with huge shards of mountains left standing.

Iceland's climate and geography is the perfect environment for the creation of large and powerful waterfalls. It has abundant precipitation, either as rain or snow, and its numerous glaciers feed rivers to produce many waterfalls. Dettifoss is located in the Lake Mývatn region, which is known for its volcanic activity, lava fields, mudpools, and hot springs, deep gorges, and waterfalls. The latest eruptions occurred from 1975–84, and the bubbling clay pits and sulphuric fumes that waft over the area are a constant reminder of the violent forces beneath the feet.

It is possible to reach both sides of the glacial river, Jökulsá, across which Dettifoss stands, although the terrain is rugged, and walkers should be well prepared with suitable footwear and clothing.

Far left: *The awesome rage with which hundreds of thousands of gallons of icy water, sand, and rocks plummets over the edge of the waterfall reveals why this Icelandic natural wonder is generally regarded as being the most powerful in Europe.*

Top right: *The tremendous surge of water roars over the lip of the fall and crashes into the Jökulsárgljúfur canyon, which is said to resemble a much smaller version of the Grand Canyon in Arizona, USA.*

Right: *The greatest feature of this magnificent waterfall—its immense and relentless power —has also turned out to be its greatest enemy: the unbridled might unleashed by the icy water has led to an extremely high rate of erosion, to the extent that Dettifoss is gradually moving upstream.*

Mývatn, Iceland

Dettifoss, Mývatn

Húsavík•

•Budardalur

•Reykjavik

HARNESSING THE ENERGY

It was long held that the incredible volume of water that passes over the falls should be harnessed for electricity, and the area was researched with that aim in sight. After much debate, however, the ambitious plans were finally shelved in the 1970s, as the basalt rock was found to be too permeable, and therefore unsuitable. The area is now protected.

Brooks Falls

Katmai National Park and Preserve, Alaska, USA

• **This waterfall in Alaska merits inclusion here not because of its size or power but because it is North America's leading site for viewing brown bears.**

• **Brooks Falls is in Katmai National Park and Preserve, which occupies the area surrounding Novarupta Volcano at the head of the Alaska Peninsula. It is 290 miles (464km) southwest of the state capital, Anchorage.**

• **Brooks Falls is also a favorite hunting ground for bald eagles, which swoop down and pluck salmon out of the water in their talons.**

The peak seasons for bear watching are late June, the whole of July, late August, and the first half of September. Those are the times when millions of salmon swim upstream from the Bering Sea to spawn. The Brooks River teems with fish, and the world's largest population of brown bears (2,000 of them live in the park) gathers in and around it to feed.

Tourists have been visiting the region regularly and in growing numbers since the last major eruption of Novarupta in 1912. For 70 years, man and bear frequented the area unsupervised but then several alarming confrontations between the two species forced the authorities to install the first specially constructed bear-viewing platform on the bank.

A year later, in 1983, the Katmai Park Service rerouted the trail to the platform away from the riverbank along an extensive elevated boardwalk system in a further effort to keep the bears within sight of the humans but outside striking range of them.

Park Rangers closely monitor bear movements and ensure that the animals always have right of way. On-the-spot fines are imposed on any human who goes within 50 yards (46m) of an ordinary bear or within 100 yards (90m) of a female with cubs. Fishing, however, is still permitted along the banks.

Far left: *Waterfalls have many attractions for humans—most of them simply to savor the majesty of nature—but the brown bears that visit Brooks Falls do so for their very survival. The falls are a prolific source of fish for the noble animals, and they display considerable talents in catching their prey.*

Top right: *A keen eye and quick responses enable the bears to catch fish midair as they leap from the water, intent on scaling the falls to reach their spawning site upstream. The fish exist in such vast numbers that the relatively few lost to the bears makes little impact on the survival of the species.*

Right: *Perched at the crest of the falls, a pair of adult bears wait patiently as the leaping salmon make their desperate attempt, and fall within range of their snapping jaws or razor sharp claws.*

Katmai National Park & Preserve, Alaska, USA

Brooks Falls, Katmai National Park & Preserve

Kodiak Island

Chignik

Cold Bay

NEW ANGLE ON FISHING

The bears either grab the salmon in midair as they try to leap up the waterfall or else pin them to the waterbed beneath their flashing paws. Having made a catch, adult bears bite off the head of the fish and strip the skin; they eat only the brains, eggs, and skin, and discard most of the red meat. The leftovers make meals for the bear cubs, seagulls, and occasional wolves that snoop around the riverbank but are careful not to come within range of the predators-in-chief.

Laja Falls

Biobió Region, Chile

- **This spectacular block waterfall lies on the Laja River in the Biobió region of Chile, close to what is popularly regarded as the dividing line between the north and south of the country.**
- **The main cascade is 115ft (35m) high.**
- **Easily accessible, the Laja Falls is just off the Pan-American Highway between Chillán and Los Ángeles.**

Most of the postcard photographs of Laja Falls are taken from the nearby road bridge, which affords an uninterrupted view of the central plunge. Because of its proximity to the main road, the area surrounding the Laja Falls attracts large numbers of tourists, but it is possible for slightly more adventurous visitors to scramble off the beaten track to see some of the secondary cascades, which, though less visually overwhelming than the main plunge, display equal power in a more confined setting.

The Laja River rises on Campamento Hill on the slopes of Mount Antuco, an active volcano in the central Andes. From there, it flows northwest and receives the Trapa-Trapa River and several small tributaries before entering a lake, the Laguna de Laja, after around 22 miles (35km).

Downstream from the lake, the river follows a tree-lined course for just over 28 miles (45km) before accelerating sharply toward the broad rim of Laja falls.

Below the cascade, the river enters a rocky canyon; this stretch offers some of Chile's best whitewater rafting. The Laja River subsequently flows into the Biobió River and then into the Pacific Ocean near the city of San Pedro de la Paz.

Far left: *The main plunge of Laja Falls is easily accessible and has consequently become a major tourist attraction. Despite the commercialization of the nearby vicinity, however, the falls remain one of the most beautiful block falls, and the main drop has a smooth, regular formation.*

Top right: *Downstream from the main block drop of the falls, the water courses rapidly onward down several smaller cascades, which are lively and fascinating to watch.*

Right: *Although the finest overall view of the main falls is from the road bridge, experiencing this beautiful waterfall from the riverbed is as if transported to another world, where the hustle and bustle of commercialization is invisible.*

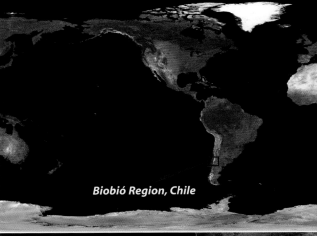

Biobió Region, Chile

- Chillán
- Talcahuano

Laja Falls, Biobió Region

- Temuco

INTO THE MIST

Laja Falls are often described as "the Chilean Niagara," and the local tourist industry does much to emphasize the similiarity between this great waterfall and the one on the U.S.-Canada border. These efforts are most readily apparent in the boat service that takes visitors out into the spray at the base of the cascade, a practice inspired by the North American *Maid of the Mist.*

Gothafoss

Mývatn, Iceland

- **Gothafoss is a block waterfall around 100ft (30m) wide that carries the river Skjálfandafljót over a drop of 39ft (12m) in Iceland.**
- **The river is formed from meltwaters that flow from Vatnajökull, an icefield covered by active volcanoes.**
- **Much of the topography of Iceland is of very recent formation; Gothafoss is only around 2,500 years old—in geological terms, that is almost yesterday.**

Gothafoss is one of the country's most spectacular waterfalls, but it is much less well known than Iceland's most visited waterfalls, Gullfoss, because it is located off the beaten track and a long way from the capital, Reykjavik. However, a visit to the district surrounding the main northern city of Akureyri is well worth the time, effort, and—a detail worth mentioning about Iceland—the considerable cost.

According to tradition, Gothafoss (the name means "Waterfall of the Gods" in Icelandic) played a symbolic role during the conversion of Iceland to Christianity. In AD 999 or 1000, when the Althing (the Icelandic parliament) decided to renounce paganism, the lawspeaker (president) of the high court threw statues of the old Norse deities over the falls. This momentous occasion is commemorated in a stained-glass window in Akureyri Cathedral. In contrast to many countries, however, Iceland's religious change was not enforced on the populace, who were allowed to follow their own consciences.

Far left: *Remote it may be, but Iceland's Gothafoss waterfall is one of the most glorious sights to behold, as the icy water tumbles in a broad semicircle from a ledge that protrudes with large rocks.*

Top right: *Two central rocks divide the waters, while a smaller channel squeezes between them. From there the white water churns on its way as a blue-green torrent.*

Right: *Deep snow blankets the ground in winter and the roaring waters of Gothafoss begin to freeze, and huge icicles hang from the ledge, creating a breathtaking and mysterious scene to the lone onlooker standing on high ground.*

DUCKS AND VOLCANOES

Gothafoss is located halfway between Akureyri and Mývatn, a shallow lake around 6 miles (9.5km) long and 4 miles (6.5km) wide that is dotted with volcanic islands and flanked by numerous craters, hot springs, and a variety of lava rock formations. The lake is drained by the Laxá River, which is famous for its salmon and trout.

The surrounding wetlands form a nature reserve and are a prime location for wildfowl, including more species of duck than any other place on Earth.

Mývatn, Iceland

Gothafoss, Mývatn

Húsavík•

•Budardalur

•Reykjavik

Manavgat Falls

Manavgat, Turkey

- **This waterfall takes its name from the river on which it stands and the nearby seaside resort on the south coast of Turkey.**

- **These block falls are not very high—no more than around 20ft (6m)—but they are very broad and have a picturesque setting among shady trees.**

- **Although the current in midstream is powerful, the edges are suitable for paddling and a series of stepping stones enables visitors to walk safely from bank to bank across the top of the plunge.**

The falls' location around 25 miles (40km) east of Antalya (one of the main tourist centers and the site of a major international airport) makes Manavgat one of the most visited natural features in Turkey. The falls follow a gently horseshoe shape, and there are pleasant shady walks by the side of the river. Further down the river it is possible to take a leisurely cruise through Manavgat and the wetlands, where the mouth of the river meets the Mediterranean Sea.

The Manavgat River flows underground for much of its upper course, emerging a few miles above the falls at the start of its final descent into the Mediterranean Sea. There are two dams on the higher sections of the river. The larger dam, the Oymapinar, is 7.5 miles (12km) north of the falls and has a capacity of nearly 66 billion gallons (300 million cubic m). Built to generate hydroelectricity and completed in 1984, its retaining wall is over 600ft (185m) high.

During times of intense flooding, the falls may actually disappear beneath the high water level, as the surrounding banks overflow.

Far left: *The foaming white waters of Manavgat Falls cascade over the ledge in a most tranquil setting, where it is a delight to rest during an intensely hot day.*

Right: *At the sides of the falls there are viewing terraces, and delightful picnic areas under the shade of plane trees which grow at the water's edge. There are also charming tea gardens, and lively restaurants serving delicious fresh fish.*

Right: *The beautiful blue-green waters course onward beyond the falls in this most enchanting of locations, below beautiful azure skies.*

Manavgat, Turkey

Manavgat Falls, Manavgat

HIGH AND DRY

Also near the Manavgat Falls is Side (pronounced "See-day," the Turkish for "pomegranate"). Although, because of thousands of years of sedimentary deposition, the city is now inland, it was, in ancient times, one of the most important ports of Asia Minor.

Alexander the Great occupied it in 333 BC, and the Romans later built a large amphitheater there. The remains of this structure—excavated between 1947 and 1966—are among the finest of their kind in the region, and many tourists visit them on day excursions from Antalya that also stop for refreshments at one of the cafes and restaurants by the side of the falls.

Ebor Falls

Ebor, New South Wales, Australia

- **Ebor Falls is a block waterfall that descends in two stages over a staggered 377ft (115m) drop along the Guy Fawkes River in New South Wales, Australia.**
- **The plunge occurs where the river leaves a platform of basalt rock formed more than 18 million years ago by eruptions of the now extinct Ebor Volcano. Below the falls, the river tumbles into a dark rain forest.**
- **Ebor Falls is one of the highlights on the Waterfall Way, a 118-mile (191km) highway between Coffs Harbour and Armidale that takes in several national parks, including Dorrigo, New England, Oxley, and Cathedral Rock.**

The waters at the base of the falls are home to the protected eastern freshwater cod, which may often be seen feeding near the surface. The rare New England tree frog may also be observed on the banks or standing tensely on the rocks. Most excitingly, early risers may catch a glimpse of a duckbill platypus, the extraordinary amphibious mammal which, though not endangered, is solitary, reclusive, and seldom spotted in the wild.

Although the Ebor Falls is the chief draw to the Guy Fawkes River National Park, that is by no means its only attraction. The area is a rugged and remote wilderness of open woodland; the main trees are yellow box, cabbage gum, Blakely's red gum, and broad-leafed stringy bark, which are all remarkable for their successful adaptation to an area of extremely low rainfall.

The falls and the surrounding area cater well for tourists. There are two strategically positioned viewing platforms along the sides of the cascade, and a rest area with cooking facilities and toilets nearby. There is also a comfortable motel, conveniently located within easy walking distance from the falls, but discreetly hidden from view of it.

Far left: *The upper tier of Ebor Falls is spectacularly beautiful, as rivulets of white water cascade over the almost rectangular basalt blocks that stand across the flow of the river, then spill down a second, sloping section before continuing down the second, staggered tier.*

Top right: *Viewed from one of the ideally positioned lookout platforms, the full, bewitching effect of both tiers of the falls can be appreciated. There are numerous walks close to the falls, and in spring the meadows opposite the river are resplendent with wild flowers.*

Right: *The falls do not always present a serene nature, and after heavy rainfall the flow can become powerful and the gentle rivulets are transformed into a lively mass of foam and spray.*

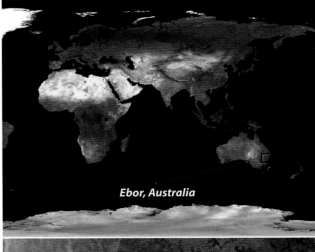

Ebor, Australia

Ebor Falls, Ebor

Brisbane •

Bourke •

Coonabarabran •

Forster •

Sydney •

WILDLIFE WALKABOUT
While bush-walking around Ebor Falls, visitors may see kangaroos and wallabies and sometimes the much rarer and shyer dingo. The birdlife is vibrant, with kookaburras, lorikeets, lyrebirds, and robins of several different colors.

Magwa Falls

Eastern Cape Province, South Africa

- **Magwa Falls is a curtain waterfall around 10 miles (16km) southeast of Lusikisiki in the Eastern Cape Province of South Africa.**
- **It drops 473ft (144m) from tableland into a narrow gorge formed millions of years ago by seismic activity.**
- **Farther along, the depth of the canyon increases to nearly 800ft (240m).**

Magwa Falls is located in Pondoland, a narrow strip of thornveld (landscape composed mainly of thorn trees, bushes, and grass) that extends for around 30 miles (50km) from the Indian Ocean to the inland plateau on which the top of the falls is located.

Although Magwa is away from the main package tourist routes around South Africa, it is popular with independent hikers, most of whom reach it along a path from the Indian Ocean through the Goso State Forest, which is full of pine trees, and across the Magwa tea plantations. This is a demandingly steep climb, but it is worth it for the amazing views from the plateau and the sight of the waterfall.

Many visitors combine a trip to Magwa Falls with a tour of the vast tea plantation that surrounds the site, to see how tea is grown and processed, and to purchase some of the finest tea. The waterfall is not far from the entrance to the estate.

After an hour or so enjoying the wonderful scenery, offroad trucks are on hand to drive visitors back down to the coast by way of a smaller cascade, the Fraser Falls. The excursion normally ends at the Mbotyi River Lodge, which has a range of accommodation, from luxurious suites to cabins, and a campsite.

Far left: *In full flow, the white water plummeting over the edge of the escarpment resembles a delicate curtain of sheer fabric. The water then continues along the length of the canyon, which, as this view from the west shows, doubles in depth.*

Top right: *When the flow of Magwa Falls is reduced it is possible to traverse the rocks to the very lip of the canyon itself—although this is a feat only for the brave. A far better view can be obtained from the opposite side of the canyon.*

Right: *Walkers approach the top of the falls from the eastern side (right of picture) and cross over to the farther bank via stepping stones in the water. Continuing on to the end of the canyon, they then cross to the opposite side where the full effect of Magwa Falls can be appreciated from the cool shade of the trees.*

Eastern Cape Province, South Africa

Bloemfontein •

LESOTHO

Durban •

SOUTH AFRICA

East London •

• Port Elizabeth

Magwa Falls, Eastern Cape Province

GHOST OF PONDOLAND

Near the falls is the Pondoland Endemic Centre which, in addition to being an area of outstanding natural beauty, features an unusually intense concentration of botanical diversity, with more than 130 plant species that are found nowhere else on Earth and one—the Pondoland Ghostbush *(Raspalia trigina)*—which was previously thought to be extinct.

Bond Falls

Paulding, Michigan, USA

- **Bond Falls is a curtain waterfall on one of the upper stretches of the Ontonagon River a few miles east of Paulding, Michigan.**
- **The total drop is around 50ft (15m) in height, and the maximum width 100ft (30m).**
- **The Ontonagon River is a complex formation with four branches that come together around 25 miles (40km) from the mouth, which issues into Lake Superior.**

Bond Falls—officially known as the Bond Falls Scenic Site, which includes the state park—stands on the 58-mile (93km) middle branch of the Ontonagon River. The river originates at Crooked Lake in Gogebic County, and then flows in an easterly direction until it is joined by the Tamarack River, whereupon it turns south.

The river drops some 875ft (267m) from the Bond Falls Flowage, a reservoir on the highlands of the western Upper Peninsula. Although Bond Falls is part of a natural waterway, its flow has been somewhat intensified by the construction of a nearby dam by the Upper Peninsula Power Company (UPPCO).

Below the falls, the river merges with the Baltimore River before joining its three namesakes—the West, South, and East Ontonagon rivers, for the final approach to Lake Superior.

Bond Falls is easily accessible by road. Leaving an intersection with US-45 at Paulding, Bond Falls Road runs for 3 miles (5km) to a parking area a short walk away from the base of the cascade. For overnight visitors, there is a well equipped campsite a little way to the south.

Far left: *Bond Falls is a particularly scenic site, and in fact although the watercourse is natural, the flow is regulated by the dam a little further upstream, for purely aesthetic reasons. A level boardwalk has been constructed so that visitors can be afforded a fine view of the water tumbling over the rocks that form the falls.*

Top right: *The Ontonagon River, and the Bond Falls Flowage, have been stocked with brook trout, a popular game fish with anglers. Beyond the falls the river becomes fairly placid, although during the spring melt the flow is much higher.*

Right: *The upper cascades of Bond Falls can be quite lively, as the water spills over the different levels of rock in the riverbed, and the sound is enchanting. Trails meander around the area, and on the eastern side of the falls there are wild areas with steep rocky climbs.*

Michigan, USA

Lake Superior

· Houghton

· Duluth

· Ashland

Iron Mountain ·

Bond Falls, Paulding

OJIBWA HABITAT

Although Bond Falls is the outstanding physical feature, the whole area is worthy of an extended visit, not least because much of it lies within the Ottawa National Forest, 1,000,000 acres (400,000 hectares) of carefully preserved and maintained woods and wetlands that were the ancestral habitat of the Ojibwa Native American people.

Dunn's River Falls

Ocho Rios, Jamaica

- **Dunn's River Falls is Jamaica's most well-known and most popular tourist attraction, drawing thousands of visitors each year.**
- **Unusually, the 600ft (183m) long cascade waterfall empties directly into the sea.**
- **The gentle nature of the falls and their shallow water mean that it is possible to climb to the top actually in the waterfall, using the rock terraces as "stepping stones."**

The town of Ocho Rios (Spanish for "Eight Rivers") lies on the northern coast of Jamaica and is a very popular tourist destination, being well known for scuba diving and other water sports. Once a small fishing village, today it is a regular stop for many cruise ships sailing the Caribbean. Thousands take vacations in the area throughout the year. Around 2 miles (3km) to the west of the resort are the famous Dunn's River Falls, which are set among the lush vegetation of a dense tropical forest.

The waterfall is almost a living entity, since it continues to regenerate itself from deposits of travertine rock, formed by the precipitation of calcium carbonate from the river as it flows over the rocks.

For years, the falls have attracted visitors, and one of the most popular activities is to climb to the top through the rushing water, which provides an invigorating and cooling experience. For safety, climbers are encouraged to follow one of the guides who are on hand and form themselves into human chains by holding hands.

At the top of the falls, they are rewarded with panoramic views of the sea and surrounding area. For those who do not like the idea of getting wet, there is also a trail that winds its way up alongside the falls, providing spectacular views of the cascading water.

The area around the foot of the falls is a popular place for picnics, since the air is cooled by the continuous spray thrown up by the water crashing over the rocks.

Far left: *Fed by springs that issue from the hills above, the waters of the falls tumble and splash their way over a jumble of limestone rocks that follow a gentle gradient down to the sea. Between the rock terraces are natural pools of cool, crystal-clear water.*

Top right: *The softly rounded rocks that form the waterfall allow visitors to clamber with safety over the numerous tiers. The overall effect of the falls is one of peace and tranquility with nature, and perfect interaction with man.*

Right: *Blue-shirted guides lead a procession of adventurers up the gentle incline of Dunn's River Falls, one of the few waterfalls in the world that can be traversed on foot. The climbers can pause midway to allow the waters to massage their tired muscles.*

Ocho Rios, Jamaica

Dunn's River Falls, Ocho Rios

Montego Bay •

• Kingston

FILM FACTS

At the foot of the Dunn's River Falls is a beautiful beach, which was made famous when it was used as a location for one of the scenes in the first James Bond film, *Dr. No.* Dunn's River Falls also featured in the movie *Cocktail.*

Krka Falls

Šibenik, Northern Dalmatia, Croatia

• **Krka Falls comprises numerous fine cascades, but Skradinski Buk is regarded as being the most beautiful and impressive.**

• **The waters of the Krka and Cikola Rivers flow down seventeen travertine steps, 656–1,312ft (200–400m) wide, descending 150ft (45.7m) in 2,624ft (800m).**

• **The Krka River rises in the Dinaric Mountains around 800ft (242m) above sea level and extends for 45 miles (73km) to the Dalmatian coast of the Adriatic Sea.**

The Krka River flows for much of its length through the National Park of Krka, an abundant nature reserve that occupies an area of 42 square miles (108.7sq km). Areas of the falls are open to supervised swimming, and there are many pleasant walks to be experienced, with wooden walkways and bridges. A long lake connects Skradinksy Buk with another enchanting waterfall, Roški Slap.

The river valley has been settled by humans since prehistoric times, and along its banks there are the remains of a Roman aqueduct. There is a Franciscan monastery on Visovac, an island in the river, and several of the waterfalls have grain mills on their banks. Skradinsky Buk, however, has remained undeveloped.

The area adjoins Karst, a region of Bosnia-Herzegovina that gave its name to any landscape composed of arid limestone plateaus, with abundant caves and potholes.

Far left: *These elegant yet powerful falls descend in seventeen impressive steps, each nestled within lush undergrowth that spills over the water's edge, to a broad, flat pool of crystal clear water.*

Top right: *Another section of Skradinsky Buk descends in steeper cascades, the white, foaming water filtering through fine green foliage and delicate marginal plants and grasses that cling to the travertine rocks.*

Right: *After periods of heavy rainfall the flow of the waterfall increases notably, as shown. The sound of the falls is considerable—"Buk" stands for "buka," Croatian for "noise"—and this fine waterfall can be heard long before it is seen. When finally the falls come in to view, they are a glorious sight, as water cascades down the terraces to the pool, where it swirls among the flow from adjoining sections, then passes on to a smaller drop in level.*

KARST, FORESTS, AND BIRD LIFE

The land on which Krka National Park stands is the prime example of Croatian karst. It was formed, like karst anywhere, through the dissolution of carbonate rock by the action of carbon dioxide and water. Over millions of years, this chemical reaction carved out the long gorge of the Krka River and the series of sharp drops over which its waterfalls now flow.

The forests around Krka Falls contain a variety of tree species, including cypress, hornbeam, oak, poplar, and willow. The region is of particular interest to ornithologists because it contains more than 200 species of bird, including the golden eagle.

Šibenik, Croatia

Zagreb

Venice

Rijeka

Pula

Zadar

ITALY

Split

Krka Falls, Šibenik

Aysgarth Falls

Yorkshire Dales, England

- **Aysgarth Falls is the most popular waterfall in the Yorkshire Dales, an area of river valleys separated by ranges of hills in northern England.**

- **Forming a cascade, the falls have three distinct drops—the High Force, Middle Force, and Low Force—spaced over a distance of around half a mile (0.8km). Although none of the falls are particularly high, they do make an impressive sight and sound.**

- **The falls were included in the UK BBC television show *Seven Natural Wonders*, while the High Force was used as a location during the making of the film *Robin Hood, Prince of Thieves*, starring Kevin Costner.**

The Yorkshire Dales is a beautiful, unspoilt region of northern England that attracts many visitors from far and wide, who come to enjoy the magnificent, rolling landscape of hills and valleys. Among the many natural attractions is Aysgarth Falls, the most famous and most visited waterfall in the area. The falls are located in a wooded gorge and occur where the waters of the River Ure tumble over a series of three wide limestone steps on their descent toward mid-Wensleydale, not far from the village of Aysgarth.

None of the three falls—known as "force" from the old Norse name for waterfall—has a particularly long drop; the highest single drop is at the Middle Force, where the water cascades from a height of only around 6.5ft (2m).

During the spring and summer months, the floor of the valley is a colorful carpet of over 120 different species of wildflower. A network of trails running alongside the river and among the trees allows visitors to reach all three levels of the falls and provides stunning views of the cascading water.

For over two hundred years, the Aysgarth Falls have been a popular tourist attraction. Among the notable visitors are the author John Ruskin, the painter Joseph Turner, and the poet William Wordsworth, all of whom were entranced by their spectacular beauty.

Far left: *During winter, and following periods of heavy rain, Aysgarth Falls is a spectacular sight as thousands of gallons of water plunge and roar over the jagged limestone rocks, the sound reverberating through the otherwise peaceful woodland that surrounds the river.*

Top right: *At other times of the year the water flow can be reduced, although this in no way lessens the appeal of the falls, since areas of the stone steps become visible—and accessible—revealing their horizontal layer formation. This view of the High Falls is from the road bridge crossing the river.*

Right: *The delightful Lower Falls, here viewed from the south bank of the River Ure, tumble between rugged rock faces in a neat, regular formation of steps.*

Yorkshire Dales, England

Aysgarth Falls, Yorkshire Dales

• Carlisle

• Bridlington

• Harrogate

Morecambe •

• Liverpool

FLYING FISH

In the 1930s, the Aysgarth Falls were popular with local children, who would often visit them to watch salmon leaping up the cascade as they made their way upstream to spawn. The height of the Middle Force made this a particularly impressive sight. Today, as a result of water pollution, the salmon are no longer present in the river.

Agua Azul Cascades

Chiapas, Mexico

- **The Agua Azul Cascades is a series of magnificent cataracts, the largest of which has a drop of 20ft (6m).**
- **The flow is divided into two streams, with a line of islands in the middle.**
- **The Agua Azul falls begin at the confluence of two small rivers—the Shumulha and the Yaxha—in the middle of a dense jungle.**

Located around 43 miles (69km) from Palenque, in the Mexican state of Chiapas, Agua Azul—the name means "Blue Water" in Spanish—is well known to tourists because it is within easy reach of the main highway to San Cristóbal de las Casas.

The waterfall spills down its course in cataracts that follow one after the other, the larger ones occurring near the bottom of the run. The water is intensely translucent blue due to the high mineral content it contains, which is deposited on all surfaces it touches on its descent.

At various points on the falls, there are places where swimming is permissible. However, for all its attraction, Agua Azul is also treacherous in places, and the current can be extremely strong: signs posted at various points, alongside commemorative crosses, warn of the hidden face of this "dangerous beauty," indicating places where unfortunate people have drowned.

However, Agua Azul is by no means the only waterfall on this river: around 500 other, more remote, formations are within striking distance upstream, but because of the difficulties of the heavily forested terrain, most can be reached only with the assistance of local (mainly ethnic Mayan) guides. The best of the rest is the Cascada de Misol-Ha, around 12 miles (19km) from Palenque, a magnificent 96 feet (29m) plunge.

Far left: *The humid jungle surrounding the falls echoes with the sound of birds, insects, and larger animals, to the extent that conversation can be difficult. Amid this surreal beauty, the waters of Agua Azul cascade over travertine stone that has accumulated over thousands of years, creating the distinctive blue coloration.*

Top right: *The phenomenon occurs as torrents of rainwater wash through limestone caves in the mountains, carrying calcium deposits downstream and depositing them as travertine on almost anything they come into contact with, over ages becoming smooth shapes resembling frozen waterfalls with liquid blue water coursing over them.*

Right: *From the top of the falls, the water cascades rapidly down its course, the vibrant blue water mirroring the blue sky as it passes between banks of lush green foliage.*

MINERAL RICHES

Agua Azul is so named because the waters are rich in minerals, most notably calcium compounds: in spring, the rocks along the banks and any branch or log that gets stuck in the stream are rapidly encrusted with bright blue limestone crystal deposits.

A visit to Agua Azul often forms part of guided tours of some of the great remnants of the pre-Columbian Mayan civilization, notably Palenque itself and the ruins at Bonampak and Yaxchitlan.

Chiapas, Mexico

- Minatitlán
- Villahermosa

MEXICO

Tuxtla Gutiérrez •
• San Cristóbal de Las Casas

GUATEMALA

Agua Azul Falls, Chiapas

Erawan Falls

Kanchanaburi Province, Thailand

- **Erawan Falls is a segmented waterfall with a total drop of 1,500ft (457m) over seven consecutive tiers.**
- **It is located in Erawan National Park, a nature reserve occupying 200 square miles (550sq km) in the Tenasserim Hills of Kanchanaburi Province, western Thailand.**
- **It is named after Erawan, the three-headed white elephant of Hindu legend, whose image the rock face at the top tier is thought to resemble.**

The six plunge pools at the base of each segment are safe for bathing and deep enough for swimming, although many visitors report being nibbled by (fortunately harmless) fish. However, few people make it to the very top of the falls—the first two levels are easily accessible, but the five above them require some tough climbing, a forbidding prospect for all but the fittest, especially during the dry season, which reaches its height in April.

The hardest section of all is between the sixth and seventh levels. Here the previously well laid-out trail disappears altogether, and the final ascent can be made only by climbing a ladder up the cliff face.

The best time to visit the Erawan Falls is between May and October, when the cascades are in full spate and there is a relatively low level of air humidity.

The falls lie at the heart of a dense jungle and are surrounded by dense bamboo, ferns, and orchids. The surrounding area is home to a vast array of exotic wildlife, including gibbons, slow lorises, macaques, and rhesus monkeys. Some of the monkeys can be a nuisance, coming down from the trees and making off with clothes and possessions left on the bank by tourists.

Erawan National Park is also inhabited by tigers, elephants, wild boar, and deer, but these rare species generally steer well clear of human activity and are most unlikely to be spotted without the assistance of park rangers.

Far left: *Set in an enchanting wonderland of delightful pools and gentle cascades, most of the seven tiers of Erawan Falls can be relatively easily negotiated, following more-or-less maintained footpaths over a 1.2 mile (2km) distance.*

Top right: *Each pool, and each cascade of the falls, has its own special charm, in a magical setting amid dense jungle that is teeming with fascinating wildlife, beautiful ferns, bamboos, and exotic plants.*

Right: *The water in each of the pools is wonderfully clear, with a translucent hue that suggests the mineral content it contains. Numerous pools are suitable for swimming in the cool waters—a suitable reward after hiking through the various levels of this magnificent natural wonder.*

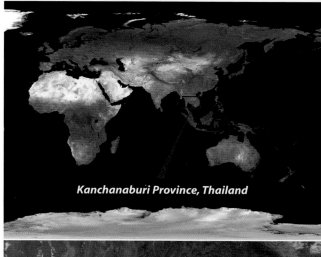

Kanchanaburi Province, Thailand

Erawan Falls, Kanchanaburi

• Viang Chan

• Nakhon Rachasima

• Kanchanaburi

• Bangkok

MYSTERIOUS CAVES

Among the park's other major attractions are four caves—Mi, Rua, Wang Badan, and Phrathat. Wang Badan has multiple chambers and an underground stream; Phrathat contains a vast array of stalactites and stalagmites and a colony of bats.

Erawan National Park is close to the Thai-Burmese border, and many people combine a trip here with a visit to the Burma Railroad and its famous Bridge over the River Kwai.

Kisdon Force

Swaledale, England

- **Kisdon Force is considered by many to be the finest waterfall in the Swaledale region of northern England.**
- **A cascade waterfall, Kisdon Force has upper and lower drops separated by a large pool.**
- **The falls are known as a "force" locally after the old Norse word for waterfall, "fors."**

In the north of England there is a beautiful upland area of river valleys separated by ranges of hills known as the Yorkshire Dales, or sometimes just "The Dales." Most of the valleys drain eastward toward the Vale of York and the great Ouse and Humber rivers, away from the mountain range of the Pennines, which runs up the center of the country like a backbone. One of these valleys is Swaledale, through which the fast flowing River Swale runs.

The river plunges over several waterfalls on its way through Swaledale, and although none of them drops over any great distance, they are popular attractions among tourists and hikers (the famous Pennine Way passes nearby). The most impressive of the Swaledale falls is Kisdon Force, which can be found in a secluded, wooded ravine, a short distance downstream from the little village of Keld.

The falls occur at a point on the river where it has cut a gorge through the limestone rock, between the hills of Kisdon and Rogan's Seat. Where the rushing waters of the river have exposed the rock, the separate layers can be clearly seen, almost as if they had been laid there by some unseen giant hand. The waters drop a distance of 33ft (10m) over two cascades, which are separated by a tree-shaded pool that attracts swimmers in the summer. In the spring, the banks of the river are dotted with the pretty yellow flowers of primroses, while ash, wych elm, and rowan trees abound. High above, red kites, peregrine falcons, buzzards, and even ospreys may be seen wheeling in the sky. The picturesque spot can be seen from a trail that runs alongside the river.

Far left: *When Kisdon Force is in full flow, eager sportsmen flock to the raging waters in order to test their skill and feel the adrenaline rush by negotiating the drops in kayaks. Here, after heavy rains in February, when the water level is high, one brave individual launches himself from Lower Kisdon Force into the broiling mass of golden waters.*

Top right: *At other times of the year, kayaking is not possible, when the water is reduced to a relatively gentle cascade, and the falls takes on a gentler but no less enthralling aspect.*

Right: *At normal times, the roaring water plunges over the cascades in a spectacular mass of white foam and spray, but after rain, the river can rise rapidly. Then Kisdon Force becomes an angry, thundering torrent of muddy-brown, churning its way dramatically downstream—the perfect lure for those in search of excitement at close quarters with nature.*

FAST AND FURIOUS

The Swale is England's steepest mountain river, and it is said to be the fastest running river in the country; its name comes from the Anglo-Saxon word meaning "fast flowing." Heavy rainfall in the upper part of Swaledale often causes flash floods, which have unfortunately been responsible for sweeping many unsuspecting swimmers to their deaths over the years.

Swaledale, England

Kisdon Force, Swaledale

SCOTLAND

• Middlesbrough

Kendal •

• Grimsby

IRELAND

ENGLAND

London •

Saar Falls

Golan Heights, Israel/Syria

- **Saar Falls is situated on the Golan Heights, officially, and geographically, part of Syria.**
- **The territory, however, has been occupied by Israel since the Six Day War of 1967.**
- **Despite their location on disputed land, the falls remain accessible from Israel's Highway 99, which links Kiryat Shmona and the Druze village of Masade.**

This attractive multi-step waterfall stands on the Saar River, which flows off Mount Hermon. This basalt peak of volcanic origin—at 9,232ft (2,814m) the highest in the Golan Heights, and indeed the whole of the eastern Mediterranean—lies mainly in Syria and Jordan, but parts of its southern and western slopes were annexed by Israel in 1981 and turned into a popular skiing resort.

Mount Hermon is also the source of several other seasonal and permanent watercourses, most importantly the Jordan River.

The falls are easily accessible, since there are now well maintained pathways with safety railings, leading from the nearby road and parking area. A rather incongruous modern concrete bridge crosses the watercourse a little way beyond the top of the falls, although it does permit access to both sides of the waterfall, approaching both the head of the topmost tier, and the base of the lowest tier.

The far reaching view from the top of Saar Falls extends out along the coast, and on clear days the whole outline of the Mediterranean is visible from Egypt to Turkey.

Far left: *In winter the bleak hillsides of the Golan Heights surrounding Saar Falls can be clothed with snow. The terrain is rocky, and the falls plunge from a substantial outcrop of crags.*

Top right: *The topmost tier of Saar Falls plunges into a large, deep plunge pool which, although it looks cool and inviting, it is not permitted to bathe. Access to the edge of the pool requires a steep descent of the rocks surrounding it.*

Right: *The water from the top pool then filters through narrow fissures in the rock before plunging into a second pool. The flow varies from a trickle of two or three small plunges or, after heavy periods of rain, can surge as a single, broad cascade.*

Golan Heights, Israel/Syria

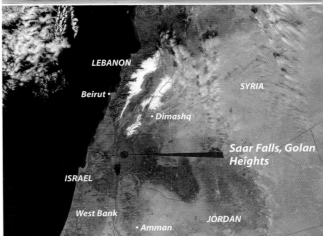

LEBANON

Beirut

SYRIA

Dimashq

Saar Falls, Golan Heights

ISRAEL

West Bank

Amman

JORDAN

THE FASCINATING GOLAN HEIGHTS

The Golan Heights is too rocky and arid for anything but the most rudimentary agriculture, but it is better irrigated than much of the Middle East.

The seasonal changes in its landscape make it a major attraction for visitors and native Israelis. The landscape is beautiful in winter, when there is snow on the higher ground, but perhaps at its best in spring, when the fruit trees and flowers are in colorful bloom.

The area is also worth visiting for the remains of a Chalcolithic human settlement dating from around 5,000 years ago, and ornithologists come to see the eagles that make their eyries on the highest rocks.

Petrohué Falls

Los Lagos Region, Chile

- **Petrohué (pronounced petro-way) Falls is a set of chute-type rapids on the river of the same name that flows through Vicente Pérez Rosales National Park in the Lake District of Chile.**
- **The waterfall is a short distance downstream from the source of the river, the Lago de Todos los Santos (All Saints' Lake).**
- **Petrohué Falls is a brief stopover for tourists on their way out of Chile from Puerto Montt, overland toward Bariloche in Argentina.**

Although Petrohué Falls breaks no records for size or power, it is well worth seeing for the wonderful backdrop—when viewed from the downstream side, the horizon is lined with a string of snow-capped volcanoes, the closest of which is Mt. Osorno (8,730ft/2,661m). Mt. Puntiagudo (8,169ft/2,490m), and Mt. Tronador (11,351ft/3460m), are also visible from the riverbank.

Indeed, the relationship between the rapids and the peaks is a very strong one. Petrohué Falls owes its existence to vulcanism: the andesite bedrock beneath it was formed by eruptions of Osorno millions of years ago. Also, low-level modern emissions from the volcano periodically affect the color of the river water: it is normally a striking turquoise, but when Osorno emits lahars—mudflows of pyroclastic material—the silt that ends up in the Petrohué River turns it a sandy brown.

Over the course of a year, the volume of water that flows over Petrohué Falls averages around 59,000 gallons (224,000 liters) per second.

The river around the Petrohué Falls is ideal for white water rafting, canoeing, and kayaking. The area is also attractive to ornithologists, who come in the hope of seeing the torrent duck, a rare species that revels in the fast-flowing waters.

Far left: *Modest in size, but great in number, Petrohué Falls comprise thundering streams of water converging at several points in a lively spectacle with the towering snow-capped volcano, Mt. Osorno, as a picturesque background.*

Top right: *The hard volcanic rocks in the riverbed toss the turquoise waters this way and that, in overlapping folds, creating a roaring white water that transfixes the eye.*

Right: *The sediments in the river, created by emissions from the volcano, have an abrasive effect on the rocks along the riverbank, and that is why many of them look so smooth, as if they have been recently polished.*

Los Lagos Region, Chile

Petrohué Falls, Los Lagos Region

Osorno

CHILE

Purranque

ARGENTINA

Mt. Osorno

Puerto Montt

DANGER IN THE MIST
Petrohue is an indigenous word that is thought to mean either "smoking place" (probably a reference to the clouds of steam that rise from the waterfall on hot days) or "place of the mosquito" (a reminder of the chief hazard of the region).

High Force Waterfall

Middleton-in-Teesdale, County Durham, England

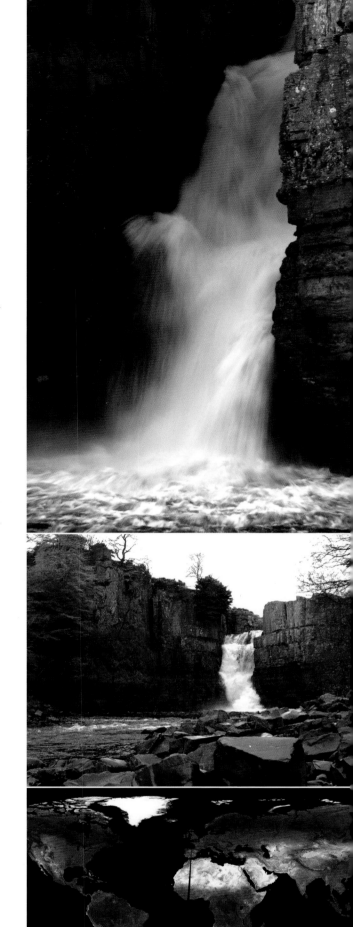

- **High Force waterfall is situated on the River Tees, which starts at the top of the North Pennines as a gentle trickle and stretches for 70 miles (113km).**
- **The waterfall drops for 70ft (20m).**
- **Before the construction of the Cow Green Reservoir in the late 1960s, High Force consisted of two separate falls, and during flood conditions the second cataract still does occur.**

High Force is often mistakenly called England's highest waterfall. It may not be, but it is a spectacular sight and its setting in woodland is sublime. The River Tees gains pace and volume as it travels toward the steep cliffs of the Great Whin Sill, a layer of which it squeezes through a narrow basalt gorge of only 10ft (3m) wide, creating a deafening roar at the falls. "Force" comes from the Viking word for waterfall.

Two types of rock make up the waterfall. The upper stage is made of a hard rock called whinstone; the lower stage is made of limestone, a soft rock that is relatively easily worn away by the force of the water. The falls, therefore, are gradually retreating upstream, leaving a gorge that currently measures 2,300ft (700m) ahead of it.

The falls change the nature of the river itself: after crashing down the precipice with great power, creating whirlpools and foaming water, the river begins to widen.

The falls can be viewed from the Pennine Way footpath at the top, or from the base, which is a popular spot for whitewater rafters. Its sister waterfall, Low Force, lies close by and is small enough to be navigated by experienced canoeists.

The woodland walks around the falls are picturesque, and resplendent with wild flowers, such as the butter-colored globeflower, the coral pink bird's-eye primrose during May and June, and the shrubby cinquefoil—popular in gardens but rare as a wild flower, occurring only in the British Isles, along the upper Tees and the west of England.

It is also possible to spot some interesting bird life among the river cobblestones, notably waders such as the sandpiper, and the lapwing, and the snipe, in adjacent hay meadows.

Far left: *A pleasant woodland walk leads the visitor to the awesome sight of High Force, drawn at first by a muffled rumble, then giving on to a loud roar as the River Tees squeezes its way between a 10ft (3m) gap. Once boasting two falls—the second is right of picture—High Force now has only one, although it is truly spectacular.*

Right: *Because of the minerals contained in the water coursing through the narrow gap, it has a distinctive yellow hue, although when concentrated in the plunge pool becomes brown and peaty, and is extremely cold.*

Right: *High Force is an imposing sight as the foaming water bursts from between the rugged rocks. The boulders that litter the riverbed have been tumbled along by the river, cast over the precipice, and then left stranded as the water recedes.*

Middleton-in-Teesdale, England

SCOTLAND

Carlisle •

• Newcastle Upon Tyne
• Darlington

• Grimsby

IRELAND

ENGLAND

High Force, Middleton-in-Teesdale

London •

LOCAL INDUSTRY

The unusual color of High Force is a result of local mineral deposits and years of lead mining. The area surrounding the falls was once rich with deposits of lead, quartzite, and fluorspar. The Industrial Revolution demanded mineral wealth and waterpower, and the North Pennines was soon populated with many mines, employing up to 30,000 miners. By the turn of the twentieth century the mines were exhausted.

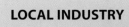

La Cascade d'Arpenaz

Haute Savoie, France

- **This stunning alpine waterfall is 1,197ft (365m) high in total and 50ft (15m) wide.**
- **The best water flow from La Cascade d'Arpenaz occurs with the snow-melt in the Spring.**
- **All year round, the average volume of water is 50cu ft (1.41cu m) per second.**

Situated at the beginning of the famed Chamonix Valley, this is a region of snowy marvels. Many of the nearby falls and lakes spend part of their year frozen, and glaciers plough their icy courses.

The Mont Blanc ("white mountain") massif, towers above the Alps on the border of France, Italy, and Switzerland just a short distance away. The highest peaks in Western Europe are situated there, an imposing spectacle of snow and jutting granite peaks.

Though La Cascade d'Arpenaz freezes solid less often than it used to—in the 1970s for example—it does still freeze. However, its south-facing location does make the frozen structure prone to collapse: a dangerous challenge indeed. Ice climbers have attempted the ascent, and some have even claimed success, but not on the basis of one uninterrupted journey to the top.

A geological feature of the cascade that has secured its interest for scientists is the marked stratification of the rock where the flow originates. Some of the first field work of its kind was carried out there by the Swiss aristocrat, physicist and Alpine traveler, Horace-Bénédict de Saussure, who was also involved in the first ascent of Mont Blanc in the late 1700s. He pointed to the rock layers to prove the transformations that have occurred in the earth's surface over time.

The first winter Olympics were held in Chamonix, so it could almost be called the home of winter sports. Certainly, skiers, hikers, and mountaineers make their way to the area in massive numbers. Among the more extreme pastimes is the ice sport of waterfall climbing.

Far left: *The water of La Laiteuse, "the milky one," gushes from a rock furrow and is tossed out into the air for a drop of 656ft (200m) before landing onto a flat ledge, which then divides it into branches*

Top right: *During times when the stream of water feeding the waterfall runs lower, the milky white cascade is often caught by the wind and blown delicately away in a fine mist.*

Right: *The setting of La Cascade d'Arpenaz has long been regarded as highly romantic. In Mary and Percy Shelley's "History of a Six Weeks' Tour," 1817, Percy writes of their encounter with two waterfalls, the first being La Cascde d'Arpenaz, "They were no more than mountain rivulets, but the height from which they fell, at least twelve hundred feet, made them assume a character inconsistent with the smallness of their stream."*

Haute Savoie, France

La Cascade d'Arpenaz, Haute Savoie

• Lausanne

Geneva •

Lyon •

Grenoble •

FRANCE

Montpellier •

Marseille •

CONVENIENT VIEWPOINT

Unlike many waterfalls, which, though dazzling, are in isolated, farflung spots and difficult to reach, the Cascade d'Arpenaz can be viewed from a picnic area at the side of the road, between the towns of Sallanches and Magland. Visitors will be surrounded by spruce forests, and may encounter the Pic tridactyle, a rare black and white woodpecker.

Howick Falls

KwaZulu Natal Province, South Africa

- **Howick Falls is a tiered waterfall on the Umgeni River, around 15 miles (24km) north of Pietermaritzburg in KwaZulu Natal Province, South Africa.**
- **The overall plunge of the falls is 311ft (95m).**
- **The Umgeni River is not vast, and may be reduced to a trickle during dry spells, but as there is so little fresh water in Africa, any source of it acquires an importance far beyond its size.**

In a global context, the river on which Howick Falls stands—known to the indigenous Zulus as the Mngeni and later rendered in Afrikaans and English as the Umgeni—is fairly unremarkable. It is relatively short (145 miles/232km), and may be reduced to a small stream during the hottest parts of the year.

There has been human settlement along the banks of the Umgeni for more than 30,000 years. The Boers arrived at its mouth on the Indian Ocean in 1824, and 11 years later built a fort nearby which grew into the modern city of Durban.

In more recent times, the falls have proved particularly hazardous for Europeans. Some of the earliest Dutch settlers underestimated the force of the water, and were swept away by the current while trying to cross the Umgeni at the top of the plunge. Between the start of modern records in 1851 and the end of the 20th century, no fewer than 40 people were killed at the site; most of the deaths were accidents or suicides, but some were murders that the perpetrators tried to disguise as another form.

Today, there are four dams on the Umgeni River—the Midmar Dam, the Albert Falls Dam, the Nagle Dam, and the Inanda Dam.

The Midmar Dam is a major recreation area, with boating, fishing, and waterskiing facilities. It also hosts a mile-long swimming race, which typically attracts more than 10,000 entrants every year and is billed as the world's largest open water swimming event.

The main tributary of the Umgeni, the Msunduzi River, flows through Pietermaritzburg. This is the starting point in January every year of the Duzi Canoe Marathon, which finishes in Durban.

Far left: *The spectacular Howick Falls is quite close to the centre of the small, picturesque town of Howick, named, in the 19th century, after the Northumberland home of then British Colonial Secretary, Earl Grey. A viewing platform offers panoramic vistas of the falls.*

Top right: *In winter the flow of the falls can be reduced, and the surrounding terrain becomes less abundant in growth, although the spectacle is no less impressive. Energetic visitors can follow an established safe trail that descends to the riverbed and the plunge pool at the base of the falls—although they must return by the same steep path.*

Right: *The power of the torrent should not be underestimated, and while access to the water's edge at the top of the falls is possible, the inquisitive should pay attention to the clearly marked "no go" areas that were established because of the number of tragic deaths that have occurred.*

KwaZulu Natal Province, South Africa

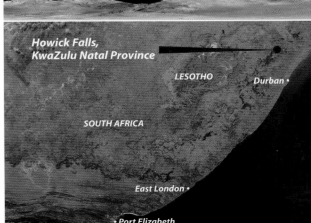

Howick Falls, KwaZulu Natal Province

LESOTHO

Durban •

SOUTH AFRICA

East London •

• Port Elizabeth

SERPENT OF THE FALLS

There are many Zulu myths about the Howick Falls, which they called "KwaNogqaza," meaning "Place of the Tall One." In one of their stories, the bottom of the plunge pool at the foot of the drop is the lair of a giant serpent named Inkanyamba. It was a holy place that could be visited only by shamans.

Spahats Falls

Spahats Creek, British Columbia, Canada

• **Spahats Falls is located in Spahats Creek Provincial Park, around 6 miles (10km) from the main entrance to Wells Gray Park.**

• **A tiered formation, the waterfall plunges a total of 262ft (80m), while the main segment has a freefall drop of 197ft (60m).**

• **Spahats is not only noted for its impressive waterfall but also the beautiful gorge where it is possible to see fascinating layers of lava rock created over millennia.**

Like all waterfalls, in geological terms, Spahats Falls is quite a recent feature. The setting that it now occupies was created as recently as the end of the last Ice Age, when vast quantities of water released by the global warming process eroded the perimeter of an extensive plateau of volcanic rock into a steep ledge.

When the main torrent had subsided, the remaining water course, now known as Spahats Creek, began to eat away the edge of the cliff and eventually cut a steep downward pathway. That is the sight that greets visitors today.

There is a fine panoramic view of the cascade from the car park, where there is a high-mounted viewing platform; a closer look, however, may be obtained by walking along the rim of the canyon and then down a steep, narrow footpath to the base of the falls.

The area features some other notable waterfalls, such as Helmcken Falls, Dawson Falls, Moul Falls, and Osprey Falls.

Far left: *The canyon walls clearly display the geological phenomenon that created this arresting landscape. Like the annular rings in the trunk of a tree, the result of the different volcanic events can be seen as defined horizontal strata. The water course then gradually cut a slice through the layers, emerging now as Spahats Falls at a midway point in the canyon's height.*

Top right: *In winter the water cascading from the falls is prone to freezing, gradually building up from the base of the drop.*

Right: *At the base of the canyon the plunge forms a pool, then overflows and cascades down the rocky base.*

LAYERS OF HISTORY

The sides of Spahats Falls show clear series of horizontal lines, and each line represents a different episode of deposition—after each prehistoric volcanic eruption, a flow of lava would stream across the plain, then cool and solidify. The process would be repeated after every subsequent eruption, each time forming another horizontal layer.

British Columbia, Canada

Spahats Falls, Spahats Creek

Clearwater •

Kamloops •

Oslo

Vancouver •

Barron Falls

Barron Gorge National Park, Queensland, Australia

- **Barron Falls is a tiered waterfall in the Barron Gorge National Park, northeastern Queensland, Australia.**
- **Its overall drop is 980ft (300m), and its main cascade is 853ft (260m) tall.**
- **The falls stand at the point where the Barron River makes an abrupt descent from the Atherton Plateau.**

Below the drop, the river flows over the last 10 miles (16km) of its 100-mile (160km) course across the coastal plain to the Pacific Ocean, which it enters just north of the city of Cairns.

The character and flow of the Barron Falls are now determined by a weir a little way past the head of the falls, and the Barron Gorge hydroelectric power station, a short distance downstream, which concentrates the power of the falls into sluices that pass through a high dam.

Behind the barrier lies the Tinaroo Reservoir, which stockpiles the waters to irrigate the tobacco and other mixed farms in the river basin across an area of 835 square miles (2,160sq km).

The dam regulates the flow of water both along the river and over the surrounding region. For this reason the Barron Falls can sometimes be reduced to little more than a disappointing trickle, especially in the summer months, when there is less water in it anyway, and what little there is is required for the thirsty fields.

Far left: *Despite the controlling influence of the hydroelectric power station, Barron Falls boasts a substantial flow during heavy rainfall in the wet season, which is the best time of year to visit.*

Top right: *The best view of Barron Falls can be obtained from viewing platforms that are reached by an elevated rainforest boardwalk from the car park. Also, the Cairns Kuranda scenic railway travels past the falls and stops to give passengers a clear view. Gondolas of the Skyrail Rainforest Cableway pass over the falls on their way from Kuranda village 3 miles (5km) distant, offering more vistas.*

Right: *The explorer Archibald Meston described Barron Falls in 1885, during a time of substantial flooding, writing that the waters "...rush together like wild horses as they enter the straight in the dread finish of their last race..."*

FALLS ON TAP

With an eye to the tourist potential of Barron Falls and the beautiful scenery in which the waterfall is set, the dam administrators ensure that the falls are never allowed to dry out. They guarantee that there will always be a raging torrent whenever a train passes over the bridge across the falls that carries the Kuranda Scenic Railway on its route through the tropical mountain ranges between Cairns and Kuranda, the nearest town to Barron Falls.

Queensland, Australia

• Wonga

Thornborough •

Kuranda •

Cairns •

Barron Falls,
Barron Gorge National Park

• Anantapur

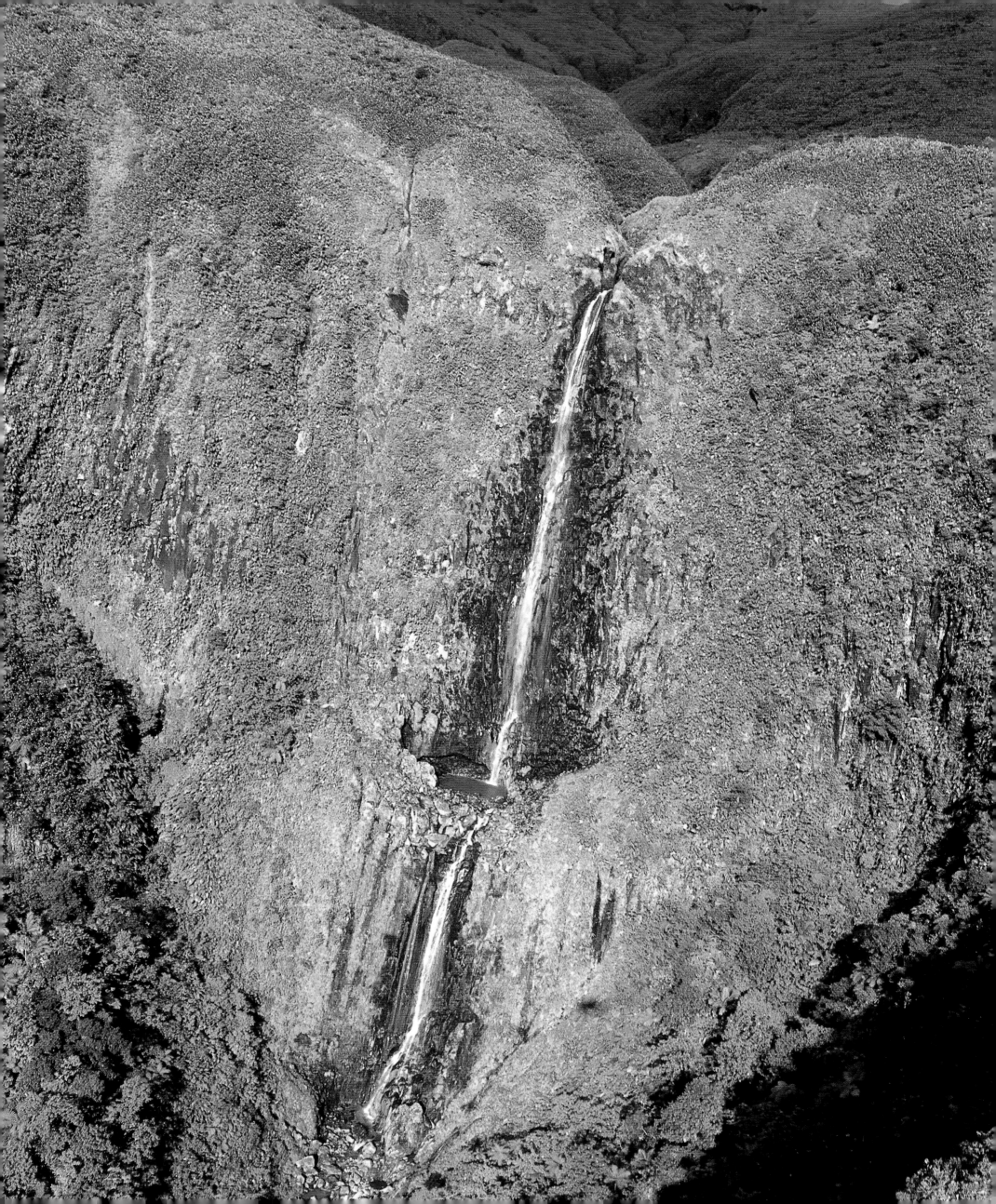

Carbet Falls

Basse-Terre, Guadeloupe

- **Carbet Falls, or Chutes du Carbet as it is locally known, are a popular visitor attraction on the French administered Caribbean archipelago of Guadeloupe.**
- **A tiered waterfall, the Carbet Falls comprise three distinct drops with a total height of 837ft (255m), making them the highest waterfall in the eastern Caribbean.**
- **Access to the falls is by a trail that winds through the lush vegetation of a tropical rainforest, which teems with fascinating wildlife.**

Guadeloupe comprises an archipelago of five islands, which lie among the Leeward Islands in the eastern Caribbean. It is an overseas department of France. One of the largest of the islands is Basse-Terre, where the geography is a mix of rugged volcanic massif and tropical rainforest. Much of the island falls within the Guadeloupe National Park, including the Carbet Falls.

The falls are located among the thickly forested lower slopes of an active volcano known as La Soufrière, which dominates the south of the island of Basse-Terre. They are fed by the Carbet River, which tumbles down the side of the mountain from its source 1.2 miles (2km) upstream of the falls, at an altitude of 4,300ft (1,300m). The first drop plunges 380ft (115m), while the second, which is more impressive, has a height of 360ft (110m). The final drop is not so high at 66ft (20m), but it is a pretty fall and does see the greatest water volume of any waterfall in Guadeloupe.

The spectacular falls are one of the most popular tourist sites in all the islands, attracting 400,000 visitors every year. There are trails to each of the falls' drops, but only one of them is particularly easy to reach. The second, center drop can be accessed after about a half hour's walking along a well-laid, paved trail, which includes a picturesque suspension bridge. To reach the first and highest drop, however, takes about four-and-a-half hours of hiking through the forest, while the final drop can only be accessed by the most experienced of hikers, since the uphill trail is very difficult, particularly during hot weather.

The route to the falls allows visitors to appreciate the sites and sounds of the tropical rainforest, where brightly-colored hummingbirds flit to and fro among the luxuriant foliage. There are beautiful, crystal-clear pools where large, shrimp-like ouassous scrabble along the bottom under the gaze of vibrant kingfishers, and rich red crabs scuttle for cover at the approach of hikers.

Top right: *The highest fall is the most difficult to reach, after a hike of some four-and-a-half hours, plunging 380ft (115m), and broken by small pools teeming with fascinating creatures.*

Top right: *The 360ft (110m) second fall, can be accessed via a relatively easy track, and also via paved sections and wooden staircases. Beyond this section the going gets tougher for all but the fittest.*

Right: *The first and second cascades of the Carbet Falls are located in stunning scenery, as they meander their way from the summit. After an earthquake in 2004, part of the cliff face split from the second fall, and access was limited due to the safety hazard so formed.*

Basse-Terre, Guadeloupe

GUADELOUPE

Basse-Terre •

MARIE-GALANTE

DOMINICA

Carbet Falls, Basse-Terre

MARTINIQUE

ISLAND OF BEAUTIFUL WATERS
Christopher Columbus landed on the island of Guadeloupe in 1493. He wrote about the Carbet Falls in his log and named the island Karukera, meaning "the island of beautiful waters."

Krimmler Waterfall

Krimml, Salzburg, Austria

- **Krimmler Waterfall is the highest waterfall in Europe at 1,250ft (380m), and ranks 8th in the world.**
- **The tiered waterfall drops in three stages, with the upper fall the most spectacular, having an impressive plunge of 492ft (150m)**
- **At an elevation of 5,530ft (1,687m), Krimmler is the highest cataract in the Austrian Alps.**

Perhaps the most impressive falls in Europe, Krimmler Waterfall has been attracting tourists for 300 years. The tiered falls begins at Krimmler Ache at the top of the Krimmler Achendal, and drops in three stages: an upper fall of about 492ft (150m); a middle fall with about 330ft (100m); and a lower fall with about 490ft (150m). The water flows eventually into the Danube River.

The Krimmler Ache is a glacial stream, and its flow can vary greatly depending upon the season. The average flow is 5.28 million gallons per hour (20 million liters/hr). The flow during the summer months can be up to 40 times higher than during the winter. The greatest recorded flow was in August 25, 1987, with a volume measuring 160 million gallons per hour (600 million liters/hr).

The falls are located near the village of Krimml in the Hohe Tauern National Park, and can be viewed from a series of platforms along an excellent trail leading from Zell am Ziller. The walk, which is steep in places, can take up to an hour, and the unpredictable alpine weather should be considered. In summer the trail can be choked with up to 10,000 tourists a day; in the winter the falls could turn into a block of ice, with the surrounding fauna crystallized into beautiful ice sculptures. This breathtaking spectacle was declared a natural monument in 1961.

Approximately 400,000 tourists visit the falls every year. The road traffic and sheer number of people is creating a great strain on the local area and residents.

Far left: *The Krimmler Waterfall is a breathtaking phenomenon, much of which is largely accessible on foot to the millions of visitors who flock to witness the spectacle—often from quite close quarters, although from safe viewpoints*

Top right: *The might of the waters crashing down the mountainside is evident, as torrents gush from high cliffs and cascade onward, flanked by dense green pine forest. From the village of Krimml the first view of the lower falls can be reached after 30 minutes' walk; from there it is 10 minutes' walk to the second viewpoint, and another five to the third.*

Right: *A total of seven viewing areas will take the visitor to the middle falls, then after another 20 minutes the finest view is afforded of the falls. Brilliant white against the deep green of the trees, the Krimmler Waterfall has an unsurpassable beauty.*

Krimml, Salzburg, Austria

Krimmler Falls, Krimml — Linz • — GERMANY — Salzburg • — Innsbruck — ITALY — Klagenfurt • — Venice •

HOHE TAUERN NATIONAL PARK

Hohe Tauern in the largest nature reserve in the Alps, and is the second largest national park in Europe. Measuring 5,905sq ft (1,800sq m), it must rank as one of the most beautiful landscapes in the world. The alpine scenery is simply breathtaking, with over 300 mountains reaching higher than 9,850ft (3,000m). As a nature reserve, it serves to protect thousands of threatened species of plants and animals. Austria's highest mountain, the Glossglockner at 12,460ft (3,798m) and largest glaciers are contained within the park.

Ouzoud Falls

Tanaghmeilt, Azilal, Morocco

- The Ouzoud Falls (or Cascade d'Ouzoud) is situated about 93 miles (150km) from Marrakech, where the Ouzoud River surges from a height of 361ft (110m) to meet the El Abid River below.
- Three major drops break off and spill over a series of tiers before they reach the pools at the base, where boating and swimming is permitted.
- Starting in southwestern Morocco and ending in northern Tunisia, the Atlas Mountains are at their most rugged in the Grand Atlas Range, here in the Tadla-Azilal region of central Morroco.

The Ouzoud Falls have a unique atmosphere, beginning with the river names. Ouzoud means "olive" in Arabic, a reference to the olive trees that line the valley below the falls. El Abid means "slaves' river."

Also unique are the shapes, created by the water, in the rock below the falls, which is sculpted into smooth, bulbous outcrops, a dusty red in color. This red earth, during periods of especially heavy rain, can turn the falls themselves a reddish-brown color.

The area immediately around the falls is fertile and supports much vegetation, but the hillsides and mountain slopes that form the backdrop are arid and stark.

Visitors can start out from either Marrakech, around 105.6 miles (170km) away, or from the town of Azilal. They will find a site teeming with life, from the mills at the top of the falls, still in operation, to the craft stalls and cafes lining the path. Barbary Monkeys caper in the treetops. From the foot of the falls, tracks farther along the river lead to dramatic gorges and caves.

Far left: *Of the numerous tourist attractions in Marrakech, Morocco, the celebrated Ouzod Falls is one of the most popular, nestled amid lush valleys, awe-inspiring gorges, and beautiful orchards. At the top of the falls are ancient mills, which are still in operation.*

Top right: *Rich, earthy colors, offset by the deepest of azure skies, and the pure white of the gushing water, make the Ouzoud Falls one of the most beautiful in the world, as several cascades plunge into three a series of tiers.*

Right: *At times the water of Ouzoud Falls changes color quite dramatically, particularly after a period of heavy rain, becoming pink to golden as the red earth is churned up and carried over the falls.*

Tanaghmeilt, Morocco

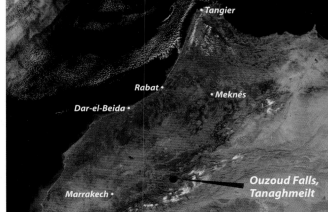

Tangier

Rabat *Meknès*

Dar-el-Beida

Marrakech

Ouzoud Falls, Tanaghmeilt

NUMEROUS VIEWPOINTS
The falls themselves can be viewed from numerous positions. The most dizzying from the top looking down! The best overall outlook is from the base, where the water can be seen tumbling from the highest point all the way down.

Grande Cascade de Gavarnie

Gavarnie, Hautes-Pyrénées, France

• **The Grande Cascade de Gavarnie is the highest waterfall in France, and the 16th highest in the world.**

• **It is located in the Cirque de Gavarnie, a large glacial amphitheater in the Western Pyrenees National Park in the southwestern extremity of France, close to the border with Spain.**

• **The Grande Cascade may be reached easily by road from Lourdes, and is therefore a popular add-on excursion for Roman Catholic pilgrims; it is also near some good winter ski slopes.**

The Cirque—which French author Victor Hugo (1802–85) described as "Nature's Colosseum"—rises to around 5,000ft (1,500m) near the Spanish frontier, against a backdrop of jagged mountain peaks including Astazou and Marboré, both over 10,000ft (3,000m) in height.

From a distance, visitors to the area surrounding the Grande Cascade can clearly see three distinct bands of rock, streaked by water seepage from the underlying limestone strata, and separated by sloping ledges that are covered in snow for most of the year. Gavarnie is a tiered formation that falls 1,384ft (422m) in three stages from the eastern side of the plateau.

The waters of Gavarnie come from Spain: some from Lago Helago, the remainder from the glaciers of Monte Perdido (11,007ft/3,355m). They reach it by way of underground courses through the limestone substrata and reemerge at the top of the falls.

In winter, the falls are reduced to two cascades, but in summer, when the flow of meltwater is at its greatest, they merge into a single mighty torrent.

Although snack bars and souvenir stores have proliferated on the approaches to the Cirque—most of them were installed by locals in the second half of the 20th century to enable a poor and underpopulated region to benefit from the growth of motor coach travel—the geological formation itself remains unspoiled.

Far left: *The Grande Cascade stands on the eastern wall of the Cirque de Gavarnie, a vast natural amphitheater, Apart from the prodigious torrent that spews from Gavarnie's source, the three great horizontal bands of rock forming the Cirque, right of picture, constantly weep water from their underlying limestone strata.*

Top right: *The scale of the Grande Cascade can be seen in this picture, where the human visitors appear like ants against this lofty, rugged backcloth. The water plunges from the topmost lip of the fall, buffeted by the wind and turned to a fine spray, before reemerging through two distinct plunges.*

Right: *A majestic view of the Grande Cascade can be obtained after a lengthy climb above the Cirque, where a vista of staggering beauty presents itself. From this vantage point it is possible to see the topmost tier of the waterfall.*

Gavarnie, France

Limoges •

• Brive-la-Gaillarde

Bordeaux •

• Bergerac

Grande Cascade Gavarnie, Hautes-Pyrénées

• Toulouse

• Tarbes

SPAIN

Perpignan •

AWESOME SOUND

The base of the Grande Cascade de Gavarnie can be reached quite easily on foot along a gentle track from the east or by a steeper path from the west. The best times to go are before 10am or after 5pm, to avoid the rush of day trippers; in the absence of crowds, the silence, broken only by the crashing of the waters, can be awesome.

Bridal Veil Falls

Banff National Park, Alberta, Canada

• **Bridal Veil Falls is a tiered waterfall located near Big Bend in Banff National Park, Alberta, Canada.**

• **It is formed by an unnamed stream of water melting off the Huntingdon Glacier and descending toward Nigel Creek, which flows into the North Saskatchewan River.**

• **Like most watercourses close to their source, the flow is narrow—no more than 20ft (6m) wide, even at the rainiest times of the year.**

The opposite side of the valley is formed by the slopes of Cirrus Mountain. The largest single drop is 400ft (122m). Although this is the only part of the Bridal Veil that most people notice, there is much more to it than that: above, the falls have already dropped 1,100ft (335m) in several smaller, but equally fascinating stages.

The two best places from which to see the Bridal Veil Falls are both on the Icefields Parkway (Highway 93) between Jasper and Banff. One is a pullover on the main road 7 miles (11km) south of the Banff National Park Icefields Center. This layby is quite close to the cascade, but the view of the lower part of the falls is obscured by trees and foliage.

A more distant but clearer prospect of the falls may be obtained a few hundred yards farther along the same road at a spot signposted as a stop for views of the Cirrus Mountain and North Saskatchewan. Binoculars and cameras with telephoto lenses are highly recommended.

Far left: *The main section of Bridal Veil Falls plunges 400ft (122m) over the lip of the cliff, but then continues on, plunging again, and carving its narrow path through the terrain before emptying into Nigel Creek.*

Top right: *The full glory of Bridal Veil Falls remains hidden within the dense, fairly inaccessible, forest through which it flows. Many visitors stop to admire the gushing main section without realizing that this is only a facet, the waters having already coursed down the hillside above more than a thousand feet.*

Right: *The main plunge of the falls is the part most people will see from the various viewpoints along the way, but further investigation is required to experience the falls to their fullest extent.*

Banff National Park, Canada

• Red Deer

Bridal Veil Falls, Banff National Park

• Banff

• Calgary

• Lethbridge

EROSION IN ACTION

Apart from its height and beauty, Bridal Veils Falls is remarkable as an example of early stage river development. Although much of the water that drops over the precipice at the top falls through the air into the creek below, some of its runs down the side of the cliff face. Visitors can already observe the start of the water erosion process that will eventually, over millions of years, carve a canyon in the rock: waterfalls, for all their magnificence, are impermanent features of the landscape.

Kjosfossen

Nr. Flåm, Norway

• **Kjosfossen tumbles 305ft (93m) down a cliff face near Aurlandfjord, a branch of Sognefjord, the longest fjord in the world.**

• **Its roar can be heard for miles around and shatters the otherwise eerie silence of the Hardanger Mountains.**

• **The waters of Kjosfossen flow from the Hardanger Plateau, which has a mean height of 3,000ft (900m) above sea level, and is Europe's largest mountain plateau, extending over an area of around 4,600 square miles (11,900sq km).**

The dramatic power of Kjosfossen is best observed from the Flåm Railway, which is powered by electricity from a hydroelectric plant near the lip of the cascade. There is a special viewing platform near the falls where trains stop on their regular hour-long journeys between Myrdal, on the main Oslo-Bergen line, at a height of 2,841ft (866m), and the little harbor of Flåm, 6ft (2m) above sea level on the banks of the fjord.

These waterways—great fingers of sea that stretch far into the Norwegian interior, and are up to 3,000ft (1,000m) deep, even at their landward ends—can accommodate the largest liners; Cunard's *QE2* is among the many ocean-going giants that call regularly at Flåm, dwarfing the quayside cottages.

The railway line itself is an incredible feat of civil engineering. It took 20 years to build, starting in 1923, and in order to make the ascent in only 12 miles (20km) trains have to negotiate gradients of 1 in 18 (55%). Along the route there are numerous gorges, spiral track loops, and 21 tunnels, all of which were dug by hand.

Each train has engines at both ends and five separate braking systems to prevent runaways.

Far left: *Kjosfossen seems to explode from the rocks at the top of its plunge, cascading in a torrent directly toward the viewing platform, where the train pauses on its journey.*

Top right: *So powerful is the crashing might of the water that the ground seems to shudder as if in an earthquake, as the foaming white waters tumble down the mountainside.*

Right: *The siren Huldra performs her seductive dance with the crashing torrent of Kjosfossen as her backdrop. The train stops at the viewing point en route, and the show is given for the entertainment of the passengers, who pause to view the incredible falls.*

Flåm, Norway

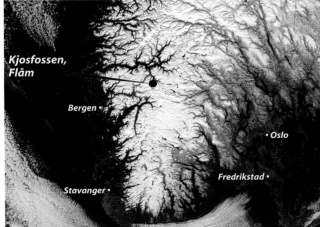

Kjosfossen, Flåm

Bergen •

• Oslo

Stavanger •

Fredrikstad •

SONG OF THE SIREN

According to an old Norse myth, Kjosfossen is haunted by a forest creature, a siren named Huldra, who sings love songs to lure men to their deaths in the foaming torrent. During the summer months, the musical part of the legend is recreated by actresses, who dance on the rocks, incredibly close to the falls for the benefit of tourists, especially those who stop off for a few hours on cruises up the fjords, after having taken the Flåm Railway to the viewpoint.

Sutherland Falls

South Island, New Zealand

- **Sutherland Falls is a series of cataracts that drops 1,904ft (580m) in three stages.**
- **The three leaps are—from the top downward—815ft (249m), 751ft (228m), and 338ft (103m).**
- **Sutherland Falls is named after the first European to see them, Donald Sutherland, who led a group of explorers into the region in 1880 in search of a new route to Lake Wakatipu.**

Sutherland Falls is generally regarded as the sixth highest waterfall in the world, although—given the difficulties of precise measurement—that claim is sometimes disputed, notably by fans of Browne Falls in another part of the same island.

Within 10 years of its discovery, the Sutherland Falls had become one of the most visited sights in New Zealand, and it remains among the country's leading attractions to this day. Located 14 miles (23km) southeast of Milford Sound on the South Island of New Zealand, the falls stand on the Arthur River, which draws its waters from Lake Quill.

The lake is a cirque—a half open steep-sided hollow—in a small rock basin that was formed during the last Ice Age. It is fed from above by other waterfalls from several glaciers and, when it fills, the excess water spills over the lip and tumbles almost vertically down the mountain wall into a valley carved by ice. It is named after William Quill, a surveyor, who climbed up to it in 1890.

Both the Sutherland Falls and the Browne Falls lie within the Fiordland National Park, which, with an area of 4,600 square miles (12,000sq km), is one of the largest parks in the world.

Far left: *Sutherland Falls is best seen either from the air, or by hiking 2 miles (3.2km) to the base from the Milford Track. The mist formed by the raging torrent can, however, sometimes shroud the actual tiers.*

Top right: *The three distinct tiers can be clearly seen from the base, stepping backward toward the summit, where the waters spill over the lip.*

Right: *From the air, the full extent of Sutherland Falls can be fully appreciated. At the top is the circue, the rock basin containing the waters of Lake Quill, which drains down the moutainside in the three tiers of these immense falls.*

PARK LIFE

In addition to these two great water courses, Fiordland highlights include the country's deepest lake, Hauroko, and an extensive temperate rainforest that is home to a wide range of exotic birds, including the flightless takahe, and the kakapo, a rare parrot. The sea inlets that line the park and give it its name are breeding grounds for dolphins, seals, and penguins.

Sutherland Falls, New Zealand

Sutherland Falls, South Island

Queenstown

Te Anau

Dunedin

Invercargill

Wallaman Falls

Queensland, Australia

- **With a total height of 338m (1,109ft), the Wallaman Falls is sometimes mistaken for the highest in Australia. It is not, but its second tier is the tallest single drop, at 879ft (268m).**

- **The first 230ft (70m) of descending water is made up of a series of short waterfalls, spread over a short distance upstream.**

- **This powerful cascade does not rely on a rainy season. Its water source, Stony Creek, provides enough water to maintain the flow all year round.**

Several tracks offer a range of options for further exploration: the Banggurru Walk extends for 2,634ft (800m) along Stony Creek; the 2-mile (3.2-km) Jinda Walk takes visitors to the plunge pool at the base of the falls; for the adventurous (and the fit), the Wet Tropics Great Walk is 68.3 miles (110km) long, linking along its route Wallaman Falls with the Blencoe Falls, on the Herbert River.

Stony Creek is one of the tributaries of the Herbert River, which rises in the Great Dividing Range, a highland region with an elevation of 1,968–2,952ft (600–900m). It then flows for 150 miles (241.4km) southeast, supporting lumber and sugarcane industries, before finally running into the Coral Sea, on the northeast-Australia coastline.

The Wallaman Falls is located where the creek drops over an escarpment in the Seaview Range, at a height of around 1,771ft (540m) above sea level.

The Herbert River once flowed westward, but changed course tens of millions of years ago, following a rise in the ocean floor. It was this reversal of the water course and the subsequent erosion that formed the falls as we see them now.

Far left: *Australia's tallest single drop waterfall is an impressive sight, as the water spills over the escarpment and plunges a giddying 879ft (268m) into a capacious 65.6ft (20m) deep plunge pool.*

Top right: *Several stunning viewing platforms look down at the cascade. At that position on the escarpment, the view reaches as far east as the town of Ingham, 31.6 miles (51km) away, if the heat haze allows: temperatures hover in the region of 95°F (30°C) in summer.*

Right: *The wet tropics region of Australia, where Wallaman Falls is situated, boasts some of the oldest rainforests, and many rare plants and animals also inhabit this fascinating area.*

Queensland, Australia

Wallaman Falls, Queensland

Cairns •

Cardwell •

Wallaman •

Thuringowa •

DIVERSE ANIMAL LIFE

The Wallaman Falls is in the area known as the Wet Tropics of Queensland—World Heritage listed as a site of natural interest. They are also sacred to the aboriginal Warrgamayan people, located in their traditional lands.

Open forest extends across the ridges at the top of the escarpment, while rainforest grows in the creeks and gullies below. In the creeks, walkers might encounter platypus, the lizards named Eastern Water Dragons plopping into the water when disturbed, and Saw-Shelled Turtles. In rare cases, Southern Cassaway may be spotted in the trees, or a reclusive Musky-Rat Kangaroo in the undergrowth.

Multnomah Falls

Larch Mountain, Oregon, USA

- **Multnomah falls is one of the main attractions in the beautiful Columbia River Gorge National Scenic Area, in northwest Oregon.**
- **The falls stand on a short tributary of the Columbia River that rises from an underground spring on Larch Mountain.**
- **It is around 9 miles (14km) southwest of Bonneville, just off the Columbia River Highway, and only 20 miles (32km) from the state capital, Portland.**

Although Multnomah Falls is widely acknowledged as the second highest year-round waterfall (after Yosemite Falls) in the United States, there is little consensus—and greater than usual controversy—about both its ranking (some sources put it as low as fourth in the nation), and its actual dimensions.

The overall height of the whole two-tiered plunge is normally given as 850ft (260m), and that of the larger drop as 620ft (190m). But there is devil in the detail: some observers insist that the latter is only 610ft (187m) tall, and that the other 10ft (3m) belong to a separate fall, which they refer to as Little Multnomah Falls.

There are three outstanding views of the falls. One is from the car park at the base; another is at the top, from which there is the bonus of a vista of the Columbia River flowing roughly at right angles to the cascade. The most popular vantage point is from Benson Bridge across the lower tier, above the controversial 10-footer and directly in front of the largest of the plunges.

The reinforced concrete arch span is named after Simon Benson, the last private owner of the Multnomah Falls, who bequeathed it to the City of Portland in the early part of the 20th century. Now administered by the USDA Forest Service, the site is one of Oregon's principal tourist attractions.

Far left: *Multnomah Falls is a spectacular two tiered drop that attracts two million visitors each year. The flow varies during the year, being at its highest during winter and spring, although in particularly cold weather the fall can freeze into a gigantic icicle.*

Top right: *The waterfall is dramatic in its full splendor, unique in its graceful viewing platform, which allows visitors to pause on their way along the trail that leads to a platform at the top of the upper falls, known as the Larch Mountain Lookout. From that point the Columbia Gorge can be viewed, in addition to "Little Multnomah," the smaller cascade which some doubters claim cannot be counted as part of the main falls.*

Right: *The 45ft (14m) long pedestrian footbridge crosses 105ft (32m) above the lower fall, offering a splendid view of the upper fall cascading from a height of 542ft (165m). The bridge was built in 1914 on the orders of Simon Benson, who owned the falls at the time, and was crafted by Italian stonemasons.*

Larch Mountain, Oregon, USA

Vancouver

Seattle

Spokane

Multnomah Falls,
Larch Mountain

Kennewick

Portland

BATH OF GODS

Multnomah Falls features prominently in the mythology of the Native American people of the Pacific Northwest. In one story, it was created by a god as a secluded bathing place for a young princess with whom he was in love.

Iguaçu Falls

Brazil/Argentina, South America

- **The waterfall system consists of about 270 falls along 1.6 miles (2.7km) of the Iguazu River.**
- **The "Garganta del Diablo" or Devil's Throat (Garganta do Diablo in Portuguese), is a U-shaped cliff, 490ft wide by 2,300ft long (150m by 700m).**
- **About 2,952.7ft (900m) of the 1.6ft (2.7km) length does not have water flowing over it.**

The Iguaçu Falls is formed by the Rio Iguaçu, which has its source near Curitiba, Brazil. Starting at an altitude of 4,265ft (1,300m), the river snakes westward, picking up tributaries, and increasing in size and power during its 746 mile (1,200km) journey. About 9.3 miles (15km) before joining the Rio Paraná, the Iguaçu broadens out, then plunges precipitously over an 262.4ft (80m) high cliff, the central of the 275 interlinking cataracts that extend nearly 1.8 miles (3km) across the river.

For the best detailed views of the falls, and greater opportunities to experience the local flora and fauna at close range, Argentina offers by far the best vantage points. With a good eye, toucans and other exotic birds can be spotted, and brilliantly colored butterflies are seen all about in the summer months.

Although geologic research proves that Iguaçu Falls was formed more than 100 million years ago due to massive volcanic eruptions, the falls are steeped in myth and legend. According to Native Guarani Indian legend, Iguaçu Falls were formed when a jealous forest god, enraged by two young lovers who fled down the river in a canoe, made the river's bed collapse in front of the couple. Legend has it that the girl plunged over the edge and turned into stone. The warrior, it claims, survived as a tree overlooking his lost love.

GIGANTIC SPILLWAYS

The formation of Iguaçu Falls dates back to two hundred million years ago, when the first rupture in the super continent Pangea took place between Africa and South America.

One hundred million years ago, eruptions of basaltic lava broke through chasms in the Earth's crust, forming spillways several miles high in layers more than 20ft (6m) thick. The Iguaçu Falls are formed by three of these spillways mostly covered by water: a larger one, 462.5–590.5ft (141–180m) high, a smaller one, 380.5–462.5ft (116–141m) high, and an even smaller one, less than 380ft (116m) high. The falls are formed in three steps by these spillways; one smaller fall and two higher ones.

Horizontal and vertical movement of the continental plates created vertical cracks in the basalt rock. A system of these faults runs through the Iguaçu region. The principal channel of the Iguaçu River runs through one of the faults where erosion has been more intense. Thus, what we see today are falls cascading over one of the largest flood-basalt provinces in the world.

Far left: *Taller than Niagara Falls, twice as wide with 275 cascades spread in a horsehoe shape over nearly two miles (3.2km) of the Iguazu River, Iguaçu Falls is the result of a volcanic eruption which left a gigantic crack in the earth. During the rainy season (November–March), the rate of flow of water cascading over the falls may reach 3.4 million gallons (12.8 million liters) per second.*

Top right: *Due to the high humidity caused by the spray from the falls, the park is rich in flora and fauna. Within the semi-tropical forest it is possible to see orchids, bamboo, and begonias growing among the pine trees and palms. The roar of the falling waters can be heard from afar, and at the falls you will see rainbows.*

Right *To get the full effect of the falls, they are really best viewed from both the Brazilian and the Argentinian sides of the river. The finest overall view of the falls is obtained from the Brazilian side, as shown, best seen in the morning when the light is much*

Brazil/Argentina, South America

Detian Falls

Guangxi, China/Cao Bang, Vietnam

- **Detian Falls is a rare example of a waterfall that spans an international border, in this case between China and Vietnam. In fact, they are the second largest such falls in the world after Niagara Falls in the United States/Canada.**
- **The tiered segmented waterfall is 131ft (40m) high and 328ft (100m) wide, making it one of the largest in Southeast Asia.**
- **In Vietnam, the waterfall is known by the name of Ban Gioc Falls.**

Straddling the border between southern China and northeast Vietnam, the Detian Falls lie among the Karst hills of Chongzuo prefecture in Guangzi Province on the Chinese side, and the district of Trung Khanh in Cao Bang Province on the Vietnamese side. The waterfall has three distinct tiers that are spread over a distance of more than 660ft (200m), crossing from China into Vietnam and back again, and being fed by the Guichun River, a branch of the Zuo River, which flows from the north.

The falls occur at a point where the steep cliffs of Putang Island thrust out into the river, sending the water crashing onto the rocks below in several segmented streams. This throws up clouds of fine water vapor, which cool the air and produce shimmering rainbows in the sunlight. In summer, the waterfall is surrounded by lush green vegetation splashed with the colors of wildflowers, while in the fall, vibrant reds and yellows provide a rich backdrop.

On the Vietnamese side, the falls are famous for a fish known as tram huong, and in the 1920s, the French overseers of what was then French Indo-China, built cottages along the banks of the river where they would take vacations and try to catch tram huong.

At one time, a floating bridge was anchored just downstream of the falls, permitting a thriving international trade between local people on each side of the border, although the method of transport was quite basic, relying on shoulder poles. Minerals, orchids, and lumber were carried north from Vietnam, while light industrial goods made their way south from China.

Far left: *The magical Detian Falls has an exquisite form that makes it one of the most beautiful natural wonders of the world. The three major tiers carry segments of the flow in graceful plunges to pools, which then overflow into other pools until the lowest level.*

Top right: *Each delicate tier of the waterfall is lush with vibrant green vegetation, while the scene is dominated by towering, green-clothed peaks, hazy in the intense humidity of the climate.*

Right: *To savor the full splendor of the falls, simple flat-bottomed rafts fitted with awnings to shield against the sun can be paddled into the pool of the lowest tier, to drift close to the cascading waters.*

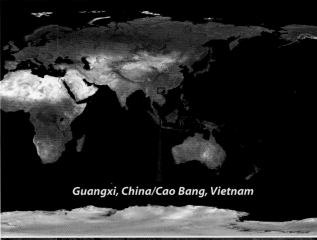

Guangxi, China/Cao Bang, Vietnam

CHINA

Nanning •

VIETNAM

Qinzhou •

• Hai Ninh

• Hanoi

• Haiphong

Detian Falls, Guangxi/Cao Bang

BORDER DISPUTES

From time to time, conflict has arisen between China and Vietnam along the border, and the area around the falls saw considerable fighting during the short Sino-Vietnamese War of 1979, which was triggered by Vietnam's invasion of Cambodia. As a result, the remote area has only been opened to tourism in recent years, following an extensive program to clear the region of landmines. There is still controversy over the exact demarcation of the border, however, and one faction maintains that the falls belong entirely in Vietnam, claiming that the Chinese moved the border marker during the war.

Grey Mare's Tail

Dumfrieshire, Scotland

- **The magnificent Grey Mare's Tail, in the Borders region of southern Scotland, holds the record as the fifth highest waterfall in the UK.**

- **The tiered horsetail waterfall has three distinct drops, the tallest being 200ft (61m) high, while the total height of the falls is 300ft (91m).**

- **Although remotely located and by no means the highest waterfall in Scotland, the spectacular Grey Mare's Tail attracts large numbers of visitors in summer.**

The dramatic Grey Mare's Tail can be found around 10 miles (16km) to the northeast of the Scottish town of Moffat, situated among windy moorland just below the mountain of White Coomb. It forms part of the Grey Mare's Tail Nature Reserve, which is overseen by the National Trust for Scotland. The remote, mountainous location, and the diverse range of flora and fauna make the reserve a popular destination for hill walkers and those who love nature in all its wild beauty.

The falls are a typical example of a "hanging valley" waterfall, plunging from the edge of a glacial trough. During the last ice age, the valley would have been scoured out by a glacier, and the stream that would have flowed into the glacier has continued to flow after the glacier retreated. The stream itself, known locally as the "tail burn," issues from Loch Skeen, a placid stretch of water that lies between White Coomb and Lochcraig Head. After plunging headlong down a precipitous cliff, the roaring waters cascade into Moffat Water in the valley below. In particularly cold winters, however, the falls can freeze solid, becoming an intriguing mass of green ice.

During the spring and summer, the steep banks that frame the Grey Mare's Tail are splashed with the color of wildflowers, and visitors can often spot wild goats roaming the nearby hills.

Far left: *Nestled into the ample folds of the lush green moorland, the Grey Mare's Tail waterfall cascades downward in a series of twists and turns, each offering its own visual fascination, accompanied by the magical sound of the water.*

Top right: *A scenic overlook is easily reached for those who want a view of the falls from below, but the more energetic can climb a steep trail that runs alongside the waterfall to the top. It is not for the fainthearted or those who suffer from vertigo, however, for although the trail is well made, in many places it traverses steep drops. From the top of the falls, the trail leads on to Loch Skeen and beyond.*

Right: *In fall and winter the lush green of the surrounding hillsides becomes muted, and the abundant wild flowers have gone—but this in no way detracts from the endless fascination of the Grey Mare's Tail, as it continues on its tumbling course down the undulating terrain.*

Moffat, Scotland, UK

Glasgow •
• Edinburgh
SCOTLAND
Dumfries •
Grey Mare's Tail, Dumfrieshire
Liverpool • ENGLAND
IRELAND

POETIC INSPIRATION

The spectacular Grey Mare's Tail Waterfall inspired the famous poet Sir Walter Scott to pen the following lines in its honor:

> *Where deep deep down, and far within*
> *Toils with the rocks and the roaring linn;*
> *Then issuing forth one foamy wave,*
> *And wheeling round the giant's grave*
> *White as the snowy charger's tail*
> *Drives down the pass at Moffatdale.*

Shoshone Falls

Twin Falls, Idaho, USA

- **Shoshone Falls is a cataract (tiered formation) on the Snake River in southern Idaho around 7 miles (11km) from the city of Twin Falls.**

- **The drop of 212ft (65m) is higher than that of the more famous—and more visited—Niagara Falls.**

- **The falls have long been a draw for people since the mid-19th century, when pioneers on the Oregon Trail, attracted by the distant roar of the water, would hike several miles out of their way to see the spectacle.**

The impressive height of Shoshone Falls in relation to Niagara is a fact stressed by Idaho State publicity campaigns, which almost invariably describe Shoshone as "the Niagara of the West."

However, although the falls are magnificent in full spate, when they measure up to 1,200ft (366m) across, the flow of water through them has always fluctuated with the seasons—it was at its most powerful in spring—and became sporadic after much of the natural supply was diverted for irrigation. Unusually low rainfall at the start of the 21st century left them almost completely dry for two years.

That problem has largely been solved since the Milner Dam, and the smaller dam built immediately behind the falls, which has controlled the water supply for more than 100 years, was required to give the Shoshone Falls the same priority as the regional farmland.

Shoshone Falls—named after the Native Americans who lived in the region—caters well for tourists, with well-equipped recreational facilities, including children's playgrounds, picnic sites, well-signposted hiking trails, a swimming area, ample shade, and boats for hire on the lower stretch below the cataract.

Far left: *The rim of the main tier of Shoshone Falls is 900ft (274m) wide. In full flow, when the supply is not being diverted for irrigation purposes, about 75,000 gallons (284,000 liters) per second have been known to gush over the falls.*

Top right: *Shoshone Falls presents an impassible physical barrier for the upstream movement of fish, such as sturgeon, and the spawning runs of salmon, meaning that the upper and lower levels share only 35 percent of fish species.*

Right: *Spectators marvel at the sight of Shoshone Falls at full water volume from the viewing platform, one of the greatest spring runoffs in over a decade, during 2006.*

Twin Falls, Idaho, USA

Shoshone Falls, Twin Falls

Mountain Home ·

· Idaho Falls

Buhl ·   · Burley

DAREDEVIL LEAP

Despite the magnificent beauty of Shoshone Falls, its main claim to fame is as the site of the attempt in 1974 by stuntman Evel Knievel (1938–2007) to leap the Snake River Canyon on a rocket-powered motorbike. As he took off, his emergency parachute opened by mistake and, although he had sufficient momentum to make it across the chasm, his machine was pulled all the way back across it again by the safety device. Knievel crashlanded at the nearside base of the canyon only a few feet from the river. If he had touched down in the water he would almost certainly have been killed because his harness had jammed. As it was, he suffered only minor injuries.

Powerscourt Waterfall

County Wicklow, Ireland

- **The Powerscourt Waterfall forms part of a private estate in the east of Ireland, although it is accessible to visitors. In fact, it has been a popular tourist attraction and picnic spot for well over 200 years.**
- **With a single drop of 398ft (121m), the horsetail waterfall is the tallest waterfall in Ireland.**
- **The adjacent Powerscourt House is a popular location for movie makers, while the falls themselves featured in John Boorman's 1981 fantasy film, *Excalibur*.**

The Powerscourt Waterfall is located near the town of Enniskerry in County Wicklow. It lies at the western end of a deep valley carved out long ago by a glacier and cascades into the River Dargle, which snakes its way along the valley floor. The waterfall and the valley belong to the Powerscourt Estate, which has a history that dates back to the thirteenth century, when a castle was built by a Norman named la Poer. The name was eventually anglicized to Power. The castle was extensively altered in the eighteenth century to become a grand house, home to the Wingfield family. In the nineteenth century, the Seventh Viscount Powerscourt turned the Dargle Valley into a deerpark and succeeded in introducing the Japanese sikka deer to Ireland.

The spectacular waterfall plunges over a steep cliff that was formed at the contact point between two rock types: granite and mica schist. It is fed by waters from a peat bog near the tops of the surrounding mountains, and the peat often turns the water brown. After rain has fallen, the volume of water can increase dramatically within a few hours.

On either side of the falls, the upper slopes are wooded with broadleaved trees, such as oak, rowan, and holly, while the lower slopes are predominantly grassland. A trail winds its way around the base of the falls, while another allows visitors to climb through the trees to the top, where there are stunning views of the conical mountain known as the Great Sugar Loaf and the Irish Sea beyond.

Far left: *The angle of the cliff over which Powerscourt Waterfall plunges means that the water slides down the rocks in a relatively thin film, which is lively and fascinating to watch, diverting into separate rivulets as it descends.*

Top right: *Less a raging torrent than a graceful, tumbling cascade, the waterfall is viewed in constant change, although after a rainy spell the flow can become more powerful, and seen in an entirely different light.*

Right: *The water, hugging the cliff face as it descends, is suddenly pitched from the surface, creating a spray of tiny globules of water that catch the light beguilingly. Within the spray zone of the waterfall, the rocks are home to many fascinating mosses, liverworts, and ferns.*

A NARROW ESCAPE

In 1821, King George IV toured Ireland, which was under British control at the time. He was due to visit Powerscourt, and Richard Wingfield, Fifth Viscount Powerscourt, decided to make a big impression by damming the river above the Powerscourt Waterfall so that the pent-up waters could be released in a magnificent display while he and the king looked on from a special viewing platform. A banquet held in the king's honor at Powerscourt House ran on for longer than expected, however, and the king was unable to visit the waterfall. That was just as well, since when the waters were released, the subsequent raging torrent washed away the platform.

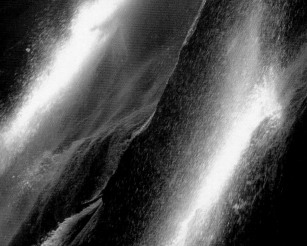

Enniskerry, Ireland

• Galway

• Dublin

Kildare •

• Limerick

• Wexford

Cork •

Powerscourt Falls, Enniskerry

Dip Falls

Mawbanna, Tasmania, Australia

- **Dip Falls is a horsetail waterfall located on the Dip River around 160 miles (260km) northwest of Hobart in Tasmania, Australia.**

- **Although never accurately measured, the falls are generally agreed to be between 72ft and 111 ft (22–34m) in height.**

By the time it reaches the top of the plunge, the Dip River has descended from 1,194ft (364m) above sea level at its source near the small settlement of Meunna to a height of around 715ft (218m). Before it reaches its confluence with the Black River, it will fall another 525ft (160m), giving it a total drop of 1,004ft (306m) over its 21-mile (35km) course.

The water tumbles over the distinctive hexagonal basalt columns, which, although can look quite incongruous in natural setting, were actually formed during the cooling process of this volcanic rock millions of years ago.

Dip Falls are accessible by the dirt road that leads from the National Highway 1 (Bass Highway), 10 miles (16km) away. In a remote location, the nearest habitation to the falls is Sisters Beach, a village around 12 miles (20km) distant.

Far left: *Dip Falls nestles in dense woodland, off the beaten track, but a gem when discovered. Its intriguing form appears to have been sculpted by the hand of man, although the hexagonal forms are a totally natural phenomenon.*

Top right: *The geometric shapes of the rocks cast the water in distinct patterns, as if each stone is like a single block waterfall in its own right. The stones that are constantly covered by the water are blackened by mineral deposits and algae, while those that are exposed to the air during lengthy dry spells become earthy brown in color.*

Right: *A viewing area above the falls gives a commanding view of the basalt columns, while there is no better view than to descend the steep stone steps to the plunge pool at the base. The area is frequently littered with large logs that are carried over the falls by the water.*

BIG TREE, OLD BOILER

Opposite the car park, a gravel path leads to a fascinating old relic of the past, in the form of a moss-covered boiler, which provided the steam power for the Blackwood sawmill, which operated in this remote spot during the 1920s.

A short drive away from the falls, the visitor will find the Big Tree, a Browntop Stringybark (*eucalyptus obliqua*) growing in a spectacular forest. The 400-year old tree is 203.5ft (62m) tall and 52.5ft (16m) in girth at the base. The tree is not on the official big tree register, but is unique in that its girth is much larger than most browntops. The tree is circumnavigated by a boardwalk around the base, to protect the roots from compaction.

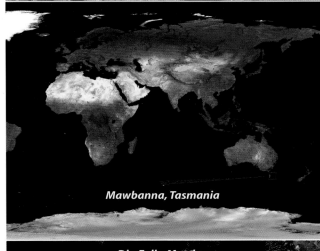

Mawbanna, Tasmania

Dip Falls, Mawbanna

Stanley

Burnie

Devonport

Launceston

Queenstown

Aira Force

Ullswater, Lake District, England

- **Aira Force is the most famous, and one of the most popular, waterfalls in the English Lake District, attracting large numbers of visitors each year.**
- **An example of a horsetail waterfall, Aira Force lies close to the north shore of Ullswater, the second largest lake in the Lake District.**
- **The water plunges dramatically 70ft (21m) down a narrow, rocky ravine.**

England's Lake District lies in the northwest of the country and is a magnificent, unspoilt region of mountains and lakes. Aira Force is one of the most visited waterfalls in the area and is located in a beautiful Victorian landscaped park run by the National Trust.

The spectacular waterfall is fed by the waters of Aira Beck, which has its source high on the slopes of Stybarrow Dodd. When they reach the falls, they plunge with a roar over the precipice and crash onto the rocks below, sending clouds of fine spray into the air before rushing on their way to Ullswater.

The park was owned originally by the Howard family from Greystoke Castle nearby, who had a hunting lodge close to the shore of Ullswater in the 1780s. They had the area around the waterfall landscaped and planted over half a million trees, establishing a network of trails and bridges so that they could use it as a pleasure garden.

Far left: *Old, arched stone bridges span the river above and below the falls, providing excellent views of this natural wonder, and its parkland setting, with its arboretum and rocky terrain—but the upper bridge is close to the lip of the falls and not for those who may suffer from vertigo.*

Top right: *A trail from the upper bridge follows the river upstream to another waterfall, High Force, although this is nowhere near as exciting as the rushing waters of Aira Force.*

Right: *The lively waters of Aira Force gush through narrow, twisting ravines between rocks that are clothed with moss.*

THE WORDSWORTH CONNECTION

Aira Force was of considerable inspiration to William Wordsworth, who mentioned the waterfall in three of his poems. In the last verse of the *Somnambulist* he wrote:

Wild stream of Aira, hold thy course,
Nor fear memorial lays,
Where clouds that spread in solemn shade,
Are edged with golden rays!
Dear art thou to the light of heaven,
Though minister of sorrow;
Sweet is thy voice at pensive even.
And thou, in lovers' hearts forgiven,
Shalt take thy place with Yarrow!

The poem refers to a medieval legend in which a young woman, Emma, disturbed by the absence of her betrothed, Sir Eglamore, sleepwalks near the waterfall. The knight returns, sees his fiancee in danger, and grabs her, but she wakens with a start and falls into the water, where she drowns. Devastated, the knight lives the remainder of his life as a recluse in a cave near the waterfall.

Ullswater, England

Aira Force, Ullswater

SCOTLAND

Carlisle •

Kendal •

• Middlesbrough

• Grimsby

IRELAND

ENGLAND

London •

Cola de Caballo Waterfall

Ordesa y Monte Perdido National Park, Spain

- Cola de Caballo is a veil form of waterfall located in the Ordesa y Monte Perdido National Park, situated in the Pyrenees of Heusca, Aragón.
- The fall has a single drop of 300ft (70m), which emanates from a narrow fissure in the rock and fans out in a broad, thin film.
- The name Cola de Caballo—which means "Tail of a Horse" in Spanish—is perfectly apt for the swishing, wispy cascade.

Despite its name, Cola de Caballo is not a standard "horsetail" form of waterfall, but rather comes under the classification of a "veil" type. Other horsetail falls generally have a more forceful flow—a fuller "tail," as it were—while this fine specimen resembles a horse's tail in such a way that the individual "hairs" are clearly discernible.

In the delicate veil form, the water originates from a relatively small outlet, or fissure in the rock face, then cascades under pressure downward. The curved shape of the rock face, and its shallow backward angle, mean that the flow fans outward and envelopes it as a thin film of water, only barely covering the surface. The water ripples down the rock face and gives the impression of a horse's tail swishing.

At certain times of the year, however, when the flow is stronger due to icemelt or heavy rain, the gentle swishing can give way to a more ferocious outpouring, and water gushes strongly down the rock face, pooling at the base, before raging onward along the normally sedate, rock-strewn riverbed.

The Cola de Caballo Waterfall is only accessible after a lengthy hike, although the trip takes in a number of other fine waterfalls set in awe-inspiring scenery of Spain's fabulous national park.

Far left: *Rivulets of white water pour down the horizontally rippled surface of the rock face, barely covering it in places, often barely touching it on its passage. The flow gathers in a pool at the base before seeking its way downhill along a rocky riverbed.*

Top right: *An enchanting vision, with a significant roar, the Cola de Caballo swishes and swirls as its stream of water gushes from the narrow outlet at the top of the falls.*

Right: *The ruggedly beautiful yet imposing walls of the Cirque de Soaso stretch up toward the blue sky, dominating the swish of white that is this fine horsetail waterfall.*

CIRQUE DE SOASO

Cola de Caballo Waterfall lies dwarfed within the spectacular Cirque de Soaso, the amphitheater-like valley that was formed at the head of a glacier by erosion.

Looming over the valley are the towering peaks of Monte Perdido, (11,000ft/3,355m), Pico Cilindro (11,000ft/3,328m), and Pico Añisclo (10,700ft/3,263m). Monte Perdido is the centerpiece of the Ordesa y Monte Perdido National Park; its name means "lost mountain," and refers to the fact that its peak cannot be seen from neighboring France, concealed by the peaks of the Cirques de Gavarnie—location of another fabulous waterfall, the Grand Cascades de Gavarnie.

Ordesa y Monte Perdido National Park, Spain

Santander • San Sebastián • FRANCE

Pampolna •

Huesca •

Cola de Caballo Waterfall, Ordesa y Monte Perdido National Park

SPAIN • Zaragoza

Virginia Falls

Northwest Territories, Canada

- **Virginia Falls is a segmented waterfall, with a single drop of 316ft (96m)—nearly twice the height of Niagara Falls and the highest in the region.**
- **The average flow rate of the falls is an incredible 9.3 million gallons (35.3 million liters) per second.**
- **It is situated in one of the most rugged and beautiful areas of wilderness in the world—Nahanni National Park in the Northwest Territories.**

Virginia Falls is a broad waterfall, with an average width of 850ft (259m), on the powerful South Nahanni River (Naha Dehé). The falls cover the entire cliff face, but are is split in the middle by a huge limestone spire reaching 2,000ft (610m) high called Mason's Rock, after Canadian canoeist and author Bill Mason.

The river originates in the icefields of the Selwyn Mountains. Before it reaches the end of its run of 336m (540km), it will cut through canyons 3,940ft (1,200m) deep, before it empties into the Liard River. The river is unique: it formed long before mountains were formed in the area, and so follows a course typical of meandering prairie rivers.

Four great canyons line the South Nahanni River, and push the fastmoving water into tight spaces, leading to the force seen at Virginia Falls. The First, Second, Third, and Fourth Canyons are up to 12 miles (20km) long, and 3,940ft (1,200m) deep. Incredibly the area escaped glaciation during the last Ice Age, and so the canyon walls remain in their ancient state, sheer and sharp, not smoothed by grinding ice.

Far left: *Set amid awe-inspiring scenery, the unbridled power of Virginia Falls is evident—only the towering 2,000ft (610m) spire of Mason's Rock is able to stand its ground, parting the prodigious flow of water into two broad segments.*

Top right: *The water flows on, crashing against the rocks in its path in waves of spray and foam. This wild, untamed environment attracts many tourists and adventurers, who are dazzled by its beauty and challenged by its power.*

Right: *The drop from this main part of the waterfall is 170ft (52m). The South Nahanni River is both famed and feared for its power, with its turbulent rapids and whirlpools. The force of the water as it crashes over the cataract of Virginia Falls creates a thunderous plume of mist and spray .*

Northwest Territories, Canada

Banks Island

Inuvik

Victoria Island

Dawson

Great Bear Lake

Virginia Falls,
Northwest Territories

NAHANNI NATIONAL PARK

This reserve ranks as one of the most spectacular in North America, with breathtaking mountains, canyons, a unique limestone cave network, sulphur hot springs, and wild rivers that attract thrill seekers from around the world. In 1978, UNESCO named it as a World Heritage Site. The South Nahanni River has some of the best whitewater runs in the world. This is a true wilderness lover's paradise—there is not a single paved road or human settlement in the park, an area measuring 1,840 square miles (4,766sq km). For all but the most experienced adventurers, accessing the park's pristine natural wonders usually requires guided tours by boat or plane.

The Seven Sisters Falls

Geirangerfjord, Norway

• **These segmented falls descend 1,345ft (410m) into the Geiranger Fjord in Norway.**

• **Its Norwegian name—Sju Søstre—means "Seven Sisters," and refers to the number of different water courses that make the plunge in parallel down the sheer cliff face.**

• **The waters that plunge over the precipice at this point originate on Geit ("Goat") Mountain behind the fjord.**

Despite the name of the falls, visitors should not be surprised or disappointed if they see fewer than seven of the "sisters"—the quantity of water that flows over the precipice varies according to the time of year, and is usually at its most powerful only in spring. At the height of the tourist season in the summer months, there may be fewer than the full complement. However, that does nothing to reduce the stunning visual impact of the falls.

The surrounding scenery is breathtaking. One of the most astonishing sights, to the east of the falls farther up the fjord, is Knivsflå, a small and now abandoned farmstead perched 800ft (240m) above the fjord that can be reached only by aerial cablecar.

Among the other spectacular natural formations in the vicinity of the The Seven Sisters are Prekestolen (Pulpit Rock), a tall, flat-topped outcrop along the fjord's edge, and, on the riverbank opposite The Seven Sisters, another waterfall, Skageflåfossen. This plunge is sometimes known alternatively as Friaren (Friar), and the local folk tale is that it represents a religious man who is attempting to make the seven sisters join him on the other side of the fjord. Skageflåfossen is lower and less spectacular than The Seven Sisters, but its waters are concentrated in a single stream and are more powerful.

Far left: *Approaching from the east in one of the many cruise boats that pass along the Geiranger Fjord, The Seven Sisters Falls dominates the horizon, looming more than 1,000ft (305m) above.*

Top right: *Viewed from the lofty heights on the opposite bank of the fjord, alongside the Friaren falls, it may be rare to count the seven distinct water courses of The Seven Sisters, but the spectacle of the white snakes of water against the craggy rock face and the lush green of the adjoining mountainside is a magnificent sight to behold.*

Right: *Passing close to the streams of water descending from the cliff top, the occupants of cruise boats can feel the spray of water as it is buffeted by the winds that flow along the fjord.*

Geraingerfjord, Norway

The Seven Sisters Falls, Geraingerfjord

Bergen •

• Oslo

Stavanger •

FABULOUS FJORD

Geiranger Fjord is one of the most popular tourist destinations in Norway. Many people take sightseeing boats from the main regional port of Bergen, but it is also possible to drive from the coast to the top of the surrounding mountains. The best high-level vantage points are Ørnesvingen, Flydalsjuvet, and Dalsnibba. The most energetic visitors walk from the water's edge to Vesteråsfjellet or Skageflå.

Jog Falls

Shimoga District, Karnataka, India

- **A major tourist attraction, Jog Falls is a segmented waterfall in Karnataka state, southwestern India.**
- **It is 830ft (253m) high and the plunge pool at its base is reputedly the seventh deepest in the world.**
- **The "mighty" Jog Falls is also known as Gersoppa Falls or Jogada Gundi.**

Jog Falls stands on the Sharavati River, around 18 miles (29km) from its mouth at the port of Honavar on the Arabian Sea. The plunge is usually reached by bus from Bangalore, 235 miles (379km) distant.

The best time to visit Jog Falls is during or after the monsoon—almost any time between July and December. This is when the flow is at its strongest and most spectacular. During the first six months of the year, the Sharavati can be reduced to a disappointing trickle, and it is said that some visitors during this period have half doubted that there is a river there at all.

Downstream from Jog Falls, the Sharavati reaches the Linganmakki Dam, the site since 1960 of one of the Mahatma Gandhi Hydroelectric Power Station. One of India's largest installations of this type, the station supplies most of Karnataka's electricity requirements.

In 2007, after particularly heavy rains in the monsoon season, Jog Falls reached an immense flow, when the authorities were obliged to open the dam. This action caused the severe flooding of villages downstream, and the destruction of crops, and great disturbance to the fishing industry.

Far left: *The unbridled power of the Mighty Jog is all too apparent from the base of the drop, where man becomes an insignificant speck against the torrent of water plummeting more than 830ft (253m).*

Top right: *Jog Falls is comprised of four cataracts, each with its own name or names. When viewed from the base, these are, from left to right: the Raja, or Horseshoe; the Roarer; the Rocket; and the Ranee (Queen), or La Dame Blanche (The White Lady).*

Right: *From the base of Jog Falls the mighty cliff soars above the heads of those who come to marvel at the sight. Shown here are, from the left, the Raja (so called because of its dignified and kingly nature), and the Roarer, which gushes from the rocks, creating a tremendous noise, hence its name.*

Karnataka, India

Jog Falls, Karnataka

Anantapur

Jagdalpur

Mangaluru •

Bangalore •

Chennai

IMPRESSIVE VOLUME

Despite extreme seasonal variations, the annual volume of water that passes over Jog Falls is massive. The average throughput is around 33,554 gallons (127,000 liters) per second. However, when the Sharavati is in spate, this amount increases by a factor of more than 200, and the highest volume recorded is 747,458 gallons (3,398cu m) per second.

Tarawera Falls

Bay of Plenty, New Zealand

- **The Tarawera Falls has a segmented format, streaming out of several fissures in a cliff face. Water from the highest outlet drops 213ft (65m), joining rapids below.**
- **The name Tarawera is shared by a mountain, a lake, and a river: Mount Tarawera is surrounded by a series of lakes, of which Lake Tarawera is the largest, at 15 square miles (39sq km).**
- **The Tarawera River flows northeast from the lake, past the town of Kawerau, then north into the Bay of Plenty area, for a total distance of 36.6 miles (59 km).**

Reaching the falls involves a 45-minute drive from Kawerau over privately owned, unsealed roads, then a 20-minute walk to the viewpoint. Visitors need to obtain access permits before setting out. The Tarawera Falls are unusual because they emerge at a point where the river is flowing underground. Rather than dropping from the top of a cliff, the water surges from several openings in the rock-face.

To approach the falls is to hike through pohutakawa and rata, local tree varieties that both bloom with distinctive red flowers in the summer. Because of this display, the pohutakawa is known as "the New Zealand Christmas tree." Native bird species such as tuis, fantails, and kerukeru inhabit the treetops. From the viewing point at the base of the falls, the track zig-zags up a steep slope and continues along the river, passing a swimming hole before finishing at the Tarawera Outlet.

The falls were created by the eruption of Mt. Tarawera thousands of years ago. A relatively modern eruption of the same mountain, in 1886, killed around 150 people and destroyed the remarkable Pink and White Terraces, which were once considered the eighth wonder of the world. Geothermally heated water created these wondrous tiers of limestone and travertine, which were known to the Maori as Otukapuarangi, or "fountain of the clouded sky."

Although it is popular with adventurous kayakers in its upper reaches, the Tarawera river is unsafe for recreation in many parts due to the hazardous nature of its underground currents.

Far left: *Like many of the waterfalls in New Zealand's North Island, the Tarawera Falls were created by volcanic activity. From studying the geology of the area, scientists deduced that an eruption of Mount Tarawera around 11,000 years ago formed lava tubes through which the river flows, and that the cliff the falls plunge from represents a halt in the same lava trail.*

Top right: *Dramatically bursting from fissures in the cliff face, surrounded by native bush, the flow from the Tarawera Falls then continues on as rapids, flowing past the huge boulders that are strewn on the riverbed.*

Right: *For some people the sound of water crashing against rocks is transfixing, helping to clear the mind of day to day troubles. It is a fact, however, that noise from the water spewing from the rock fissures, can be quite deafening.*

Bay of Plenty, New Zealand

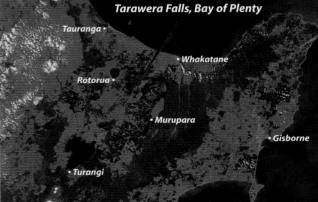

Tarawera Falls, Bay of Plenty

Tauranga
Whakatane
Rotorua
Murupara
Gisborne
Turangi

THE GHOST CANOE

Before the eruption of Mount Tarawera in 1886, which drastically altered many of the surrounding lakes in the area, a boat full of tourists, who were returning from visiting the Pink and White Terraces, saw a Maori war canoe approach their vessel only to disappear again mysteriously. Nine days later the devastating eruption occurred. Tribal elders called the phenomenon a waka wairua, a spirit canoe. They believe that the canoe will appear as a warning if the mountain is going to erupt again.

Garganta del Diablo

Argentina/Brazil, South America

- **The Garganta del Diablo forms a segment of the Iguaçu Falls. Its name in English means "devil's throat."**
- **It stands on the Iguazu River, 14 miles (23km) above its confluence with the Paraná River in northern Patagonia.**
- **Of all the 275 cascades that comprise the world-renowned Iguaçu Falls, the Garganta del Diablo is the most celebrated.**

The Garganta del Diablo is horseshoe-shaped, around 500ft (150m) wide and 1,100ft (335m) high. Two-thirds of the Garganta are in Argentine territory; the remainder is in neighboring Brazil.

Because there are protruding ledges within the semicircular chasm, the falling torrents create a mass of spray that can reach up to 500ft (150m) in the air and in turn produce hundreds of rainbows.

When the mists clear, the ledges of the falls reveal a host of flora, including Podostemaceae, a family of water plants that grow only in fast-flowing torrents.

Garganta del Diablo may be reached from either of the countries that border it. The best access to the foot of the canyon is along a specially constructed walkway from the Brazilian side. Visitors who want to see the top of the falls should approach from the Argentine side, either by miniature electric railway—*el tren ecologico de la selva* (the ecological jungle train)—or in one of the motorized golf carts that may be hired and driven along a dirt road that runs parallel to the track. There is also wheelchair access.

The surrounding rainforest is a conservation area full of bamboos, palms, creepers, and numerous other species of tree, from the tropical to the semi-deciduous.

Far left: *The massive volume of water surging into the narrow, semicircular chasm known as the Devil's Throat, creates an effect that has been likened to that of "an ocean plunging into an abyss." Garganta del Diablo is an awesome sight from the air, but just as impressive when viewed from the the base of the canyon itself—the walkway, bottom of picture, leads from the Brazilian side to present a view into the capacious maw itself.*

Top right: *From the observation platform one can stare directly into the curve of the horseshoe—to the deafening accompaniment of the broiling waters—and see voluminous clouds of spray that can ascend to incredible heights.*

Right: *From the top of the horseshoe on the Argentine side, the Devil's Throat can be witnessed from a close range. The water, in the main, is pure white, but stained with yellow where silt is washed over the edge of the falls.*

WATERFALL WILDLIFE
Among the animals that visitors are most likely to see is the iguana. Deer and tapir may sometimes be glimpsed, and some lucky tourists have observed ocelots and jaguars. There is also a host of birds, notably toucans. The turbulent waters above and below the falls are home to acará cascudo, golden salmon, and mandi.

Brazil/Argentina, South America

Cascavel

Curitiba

Foz do Iguaçu

PARAGUAY

Chapecó

ARGENTINA

BRAZIL

Garganta del Diablo, Paraná/Misiones

Porto Alegre

Cascades de Trou de Fer

Réunion Island, Indian Ocean

- **This tiered segmented waterfall on the island of Réunion in the Indian Ocean has four drops over a total height of 2,380ft (725m).**

- **Trou de Fer—French for "iron hole"—lies on the Bras de Caverne River, which starts in a mountainside cirque (a lake formed by glacial action) and then plummets almost immediately into two small consecutive falls, and then into a third, which is 1,000ft (300m) high.**

- **At the base of this stage, the torrent slows over a reduced gradient before plunging down another 1,000ft (300m) drop.**

The Cascades de Trou de Fer is the largest and most spectacular of the numerous waterfalls found on Réunion. The island is a French overseas department, 40 miles (65km) long and 30 miles (50km) wide. It is located about 400 miles (640km) east of Madagascar, and 110 miles (177km) southwest of Mauritius. Originally formed by volcanic activity, it still has an active crater, the Piton de la Fournaise, on Le Volcan, a peak near the east coast.

The island's modern landscape is characterized by steep mountains. The tallest is Piton des Nieges (10,069 ft/3,069m), and there are two other peaks of over 9,000ft (2,740m). These great summits are dissected by short, torrential rivers.

The Iron Hole, extremely inaccessible on foot, comprises a circular wall—about a thousand feet (300m) across—with numerous waterfalls pouring over it from various feeder canyons; not all the falls flow throughout the year. The main fall, however, located adjacent to smaller, but still powerful twin falls, is the one that flows from the Bras de Caverne River.

Below the magnificent cascade, the river then jumps another 80ft (24m) at the entrance to a narrow slot canyon, known as the "Corridor," which extends for more than 2 miles (3km) downstream.

Far left: *It is hard to imagine the sheer scale of the Trou de Fer, when it is considered that this aerial picture shows only the final 1,000ft (300m) drop. The main fall, right of picture, has already plunged in three magnificent tiers.*

Top right: *Having already dropped more than 1,000ft (300m), the falls, fed by smaller springs and side canyons, take their final plunge into the abyss.*

Right: *The final cascade pours into a plunge pool, which then overflows an 80ft (24m) ledge into a dark, damp slot canyon.*

Cirque de Salazie, Réunion

Saint-Denis

Saint-Paul

Salazie

Saint-Pierre

Trou de Fer,
Cirque de Salazie

INTO THE HELL HOLE

The full height of the Trou de Fer is popular with canyoners, who spend three days rappelling down the steep, slippery walls, close to the main waterfall, before entering the slot canyon at the very base, and then hiking for two hours on a jungle track to an exit point of what some describe as the "hell hole."

The Trou de Fer is known to be a very dangerous canyon to traverse. With 20ft (6m) of rain per year, the porous rock can be incredibly loose and slippery. Rockfalls are also a real danger, and immense skill is required on the part of the canyoners. Sadly, a substantial number of people have lost their lives in the last decade.

Låtefossen

Odda Valley, Norway

• **One of the most famous sights in Scandinavia, Låtefossen is a glorious segmented waterfall that plummets 459ft (140m) down the side of a mountain in western Norway.**

• **This is generally regarded as the finest of a host of cascades located in the Odda Valley (Oddadalen).**

• **Låtefossen is easily accessible by road from Bergen, the nearest city, and may also be reached on foot or by off-road motor vehicle from the banks of the Hardangerfjord.**

What makes Låtefossen unique is that its source, Lotevatnet, the lake immediately above the cliff, has two outlets, side by side; the two streams of water start off in parallel but then merge into a single cascade about halfway down the mountainside before they hit the river on the valley floor, and merge with another river.

Some of the bedrock over which Låtefossen flows dates from the Precambrian Period, between around 4 billion and 542 million years ago: this is as old as any known geological formation in the world. Normally concealed beneath subsequent depositions, these rocks were uncovered by the vast amounts of water erosion that took place at the end of the last Ice Age. It was during this great climate change, around 10,000 years ago, that Låtefossen was probably formed.

Waterfalls and hydropower figure significantly in the area. The Norwegian Hydropower and Industrial Musuem maintains the dramatic history of waterfalls, in addition to the spread of international tourism to the region, the worker' culture, the art of engineering, and how electricity changed the face of Norway.

Far left: *An impossible force to ignore, and an imposing phenomenon to confront with just a camera, one of the mighty pair of Låtefossen's cascades explodes down the mountainside, headed directly toward a viewpoint on the stone bridge that dares to cross its path.*

Top right: *The twin streams of Låtefossen thunder down the mountainside in parallel before merging into a single cascade immediately after surging beneath the six stone arches of the sturdy road bridge.*

Right: *Gushing under the low arches of the bridge, the streams become one, then promptly join another river, which surges onward to the left.*

VALLEY OF WATERFALLS

The Odda Valley is a vast ravine between the Hardangervidda plateau and the Folgefonna glacier. Among the other highlights of the so-called Valley of the Waterfalls are Espelandfoss, Strandfoss, Tjørnadalsfoss, and Vidfoss, created by meltwater from the glacier, and all within a distance of 6.2 miles (10km).

The Odda Valley covers an area of 646.3 square miles (1,673sq km), and 7,400 inhabitants. It was, during the 19th century, one of the most popular areas for tourism, brought by the cruise ships. The glacier, just west of Odda, is the largest in Europe.

Odda Valley, Norway

Låtefossen, Odda Valley

• Oslo

Fredrikstad •

Stavanger •

Hogenakal Falls

Tamil Nadu, India

• **Hogenakal Falls is a segmented waterfall on the Cauvery River, a sacred waterway in Tamil Nadu, India. Its biggest drop is 65ft (20m).**

• **The falls mark the point at which the Cauvery leaves its steepest section and flows into the plain formed by its delta on the final approach to the sea.**

• **The river enters the Bay of Bengal to the south of Cuddalore at the end of its spectacular 475-mile (765km) journey from Brahmagiri Hill in the Western Ghats mountain range.**

Hogenakal Falls is around 30 miles (48km) west of the market town of Dharmapuri. Most visitors reach it from Bangalore, around 80 miles (130km) away, a two-and-a-half-hour journey by bus or taxi.

The Hogenakal Falls are popular not only for their great beauty but also because they are one of the region's main points of embarkation onto the waters, which are believed to have great healing properties.

Above the falls, much of the Cauvery's course has been through wild, twisted gorges that are almost inaccessible. But just before Hogenakal, the river enters a wooded valley in which its course is dotted with rocky outcrops and towering trees in midstream. These mark the start of the rapids that lead into the falls themselves.

Having taken the leap, the Cauvery seems to take stock of its long and tortuous journey so far, and thousands of pilgrims take advantage of the calm stretch to take trips out into midstream in coracles with hulls made of buffalo hide or black plastic sheeting. The boatmen take their vessels alarmingly close to the torrent, well within the splash zone, so that their passengers can wet themselves without full immersion.

Not that full immersion is necessarily unsafe: local boys gather on the rocks beside the plunge pool and offer diving exhibitions to pilgrims and tourists for a small fee per leap. The water here is thought to be around 100ft (30m) deep.

Far left: *The gorge though which Hogenakal Falls flows is, during the rainy season, a ferocious torrent. During the dry season the waters recede enough for 8ft (2.4m) diameter coracles to be taken into the waterway and up to the cascades, so passengers can partially immerse themselves in the spray.*

Top right: *The waters of Hokenakal Falls, on their journey to the gorge, pass through a forest which contains herbs believed to be beneficial to the health, making bathing curative.*

Right: *Developments are underway at Hogenakal Falls, by the Tamil Nadu government, to provide safe drinking water for the urban and rural areas of the surrounding districts. This beautiful area, therefore, provides a magnificent vista to visitors, in addition to possible improvements for the local community.*

SACRED WATERS
There are many other holy sites on the Cauvery, whose entire length is sacred; the river is known to Hindus as Daksina Ganga, "the Ganges of the South." In the lower course of the river is Srirangam Island, a major center of pilgrimage. However, Hogenakal is one of the farthest upstream shrines.

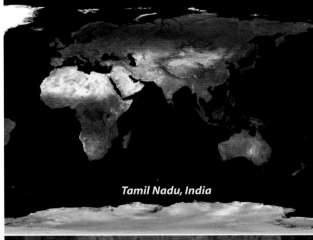

Tamil Nadu, India

Hogenakal Falls, Tamil Nadu

• Bangalore

• Salem

Chalakudi •

• Madurai

Wailua Falls

Kauai Island, Hawaii, USA

- **Wailua Falls is a horsetail cascade on Kauai, the so-called "Garden Isle" of Hawaii. It is one of the most easily accessible waterfalls in the whole of the 50th State.**

- **Although some authorities (including the most popular local guidebook) claim that the plunge is 173ft (52.7m) tall, it certainly looks closer to the official height of 80ft (24m). However, its size is a minor consideration; what makes the falls attractive is its immense tropical beauty.**

- **For the greater part of the year, the waters of Wailua Falls flow in three distinct, parallel segments, but during the rainy season these may amalgamate into a single, raging torrent.**

The falls are fed by the Wailua River, which flows for around 10 miles (16km) from the slopes of the central Mount Waialeale (5,148 ft/1,569m) to the coast of the Pacific Ocean.

There are pathways down either side of the falls, but the local authorities discourage their use because they are slippery and potentially dangerous. (Kauai is generally regarded as the wettest place on Earth.) Such strictures do not deter all visitors, however. Neither are attempts to stop people swimming in the plunge pool entirely successful, but this, too, is a hazardous recreation because of the strong currents.

Apart from the falls, the main point of interest along the Wailua River is a lava cave overgrown with lush vegetation and curtained by a smaller cascade. This formation is known as the Fern Grotto.

The name Wailua comes from the Hawaiian for "two waters," and probably refers to the confluence of a smaller stream with the main river around 2 miles (3km) from the sea. In ancient times is is said that warriors would leap from the top of the falls in order to prove their bravery. Nowadays jumping is strictly forbidden, as is the somewhat arduous hike to the top of the falls.

Far left: *A convenient lookout point affords the best, and safest, view of Wailua Falls, without the need to hike, since the terrain around the site is notoriously wet and slippery. From the vantage point it is easy to see how the rocky flat top of the falls has been gouged with channels by centuries of flowing water.*

Top right: *The falls change dramatically in appearance, depending upon rainfall and the river's flow. The best time of day to view the falls is early in the morning as the sun reflects from the cascading water.*

Right: *A slippery trail leads down to the base of the falls, where many people are tempted to take a dip in the cool mountain water—although this is discouraged by the authorities, since the currents in the plunge pool can be fierce.*

Kauai, Hawaii, USA

Wailua Falls, Kauai

KAUAI

OAHU

Honolulu

MAUI

HAWAII

TAHITI TO TV

The surrounding area is part of the Wailua State Park, a 1,100-acre (450 hectare) reserve that occupies the site of the earliest known human settlement on Kauai, which occurred as recently as the 12th century when migrants arrived by boat from Tahiti.

The Wailua Falls are best known from their appearance on the pre-title sequence of *Fantasy Island*, a popular television adventure series that ran from 1978 to 1984.

Niagara Falls

New York State, U.S.A/Ontario, Canada

- **From the 18th century, the immense power and beauty of the Niagara Falls has attracted swarms of tourists to the border of Canada and the United States, northwest of Buffalo and southwest of Toronto.**
- **The falls are divided into two sections. On the US side are the American Falls, 190ft (58m) high and 1,050ft (320m) wide, including the smaller Bridal Veil Falls, which are separated from the main cataract by Luna Island.**
- **On the Canadian side, the Horseshoe Falls plunge from a height of 183.7ft (56m), and course along a wider length of 2,198ft (670 m).**

Niagara Falls presents a multitude of options to visitors. Prospect Point and Terrapin Point on the U.S. side, and Queen Victoria Park on the Canadian side, provide good views, as does the Rainbow Bridge, which joins the towns of Niagara Falls, New York and Niagara Falls, Ontario, 1,000ft (300m) downstream from the cataracts.

Many waterfall experiences are on offer. The "Journey Behind the Falls" leads them into tunnels under the Horseshoe Falls. Elevators travel up and down, aircraft fly overhead, and observation towers loom. At night, the Horsehoe Falls are lit by multicolored beams. In the international waterfall community, the Niagara Falls is an A-list celebrity.

None of the razzmatazz would be possible if not for the magnificent Niagara River, 12,000 years old, which flows for 35 miles (56.3km) from Lake Erie to Lake Ontario. The falls occur halfway between the two. Below them is the Niagara Gorge, forged over the course of 7,000 years by the recession of the falls, caused by erosion of the dolomite and shale strata. This process has been slowed by the diversion of water upstream for hydroelectric power, and by fortification work that took place in 1969, when the flow was shut off altogether for a period.

Far left: *Helicopters and light aircraft make their way high overhead, offering an astonishing bird's eye view of Niagara Falls. From the air the Horseshoe Falls appear like an ocean emptying away—yet the flow never ceases.*

Top right: *The American Falls alone cast a jaw dropping volume of water alone over their crest, shown here with the Horseshoe Falls in the background, separated by Luna Island. Although the flow is now controlled by weirs and tunnels upstream, some 45 million gallons (170 million liters) of water surge over the combined falls in peak tourist hours.*

Right: *One of the most popular ways to experience Niagara Falls is to take the famous "Maid of the Mist" boat trip, which ferries passengers directly into the spray of the Horseshoe Falls. From this close range one can appreciate something of the incredible force of the water, and—despite the blue plastic capes—receive a thorough but exhilarating soaking.*

FLOW OF HUMANITY

The unique Niagara cascades have attracted many equally unique characters over the centuries. The Seneca Indians inhabited the region originally. French explorers, missionaries, and a Scandinavian naturalist were among the first Europeans to record their arrival.

Since then, honeymooners and film crews have taken their place beside daredevils such as Annie Taylor, who was the first person to go over the falls in a barrel in 1901. She had this to say when she emerged: "No one should ever try that again." But they have, risking limb, life, and criminal charges.

In 1960, a 7-year-old boy even survived an accidental tumble over Horseshoe Falls, protected by only a life-preserver vest. This roaring current of humanity looks set to continue, with 20 million people expected to visit in 2008 alone.

New York State, USA/Ontario, Canada

Niagara Falls, New York State/Ontario

Lake Huron

Kingston

Toronto · Lake Ontario

Hamilton ·

· Buffalo

Detroit · Lake Erie

· Cleveland

Chitrakot Falls

Bastar, Chhattisgarth, India

- **Chitrakot Falls is the widest waterfall in India. During the monsoon season (July–October), its waters swell to more than 1,000ft (300m) across.**
- **The main plunge is 100ft (30m) in height.**
- **The horseshoe falls are located around 30 miles (48km) from the city of Jagdalpur in the central state of Madhya Pradesh.**

Chitrakot Falls stands on the Indravati River, a tributary of the Godavari. The Indravati flows in a generally westerly direction from its source in the Eastern Ghats mountain range in the state of Orissa. The falls themselves are within Bastar, a district of Chhattisgarth state in central India, of which Jagdalpur is the district headquarters. A large part of Bastar is clothed in forests containing trees such as seesam, sal, bamboo, and teak. It is the region's wonderful lakes and waterfalls that attracts tourists.

Although there are a couple of hotels and restaurants in the immediate vicinity, Chitrakot Falls are not well geared to tourism and are practically accessible only by a small road (there is also a helipad, but that is used almost exclusively by government officials).

Nevertheless, Chitrakot Falls attracts a small but steady flow of tourists, most of whom come to the area principally to see the wildlife: the heavily forested banks of the Indravati River are a nature reserve dedicated to the preservation of the tiger.

The falls themselves are mesmerizing, particularly at night, when the area is artificially illuminated.

Far left: *During the monsoon season Chitrakot Falls achieves its full flow, and takes on a dramatic golden color, caused by the presence of silt, which is churned up during flooding. In the summer the water level recedes substantially. In the morning the water can appear milky white, turning reddish as the sun sets.*

Top right: *High humidity causes mist to form around the falls, which adds to the mystique of the falls, although quiet contemplation is not always easy with the crashing sound of the water ever present.*

Right: *The raging torrent tumbles 100ft (30m) over the edge of the horseshoe rim of the falls, and then becomes surprisingly calmer, and boatmen then take to the waters of this broad river.*

Bastar, India

Chandraur •

Chitrakot Falls, Bastar

• Jagdalpur

• Malakanagiri

Hyderabad •

• Kakinada

Vijaywada •

BIG CAT RESERVE

The Indravati Reserve occupies an area of 1,081 square miles (2,800sq km) and contains some of India's finest mixed (moist and dry) deciduous forests that are among the tiger's favorite habitats. However, sightings of the big cats are rare, and as a result the effectiveness of the reserve has been questioned by some commentators, especially lobbyists who want to dam the river higher up and turn the whole district into a reservoir.

Nevertheless, the area remains of great interest to naturalists because of the abundance of several of the tiger's prey species, including wild boar, buffalo, and several types of deer.

Blue Nile Falls

Amhara, Ethiopia

• **At their full volume in the rainy season, which runs from June to September, the Blue Nile Falls span a width of 1,312ft (400m). The drop is around 147ft (45m).**

• **The majority of the water feeding the four streams of the falls is now diverted to a hydroelectric plant. Visitors can see them in full flow only on specific days, currently for one day per week.**

• **Much chronicled throughout history, the Blue Nile River is traditionally thought to rise in a spring near Lake Tana, the largest lake in Ethiopia.**

One feature of the Blue Nile Falls in particular drew comment from an early European visitor. In search of the source of the Nile, the Scottish traveler and writer, James Bruce, in 1770, wrote, "A thick fume, or haze, covered the fall all around, and hung over the course of the stream both above and below, marking its track, though the water was not seen... It was a most magnificent sight."

This mist referred to by Bruce gave the falls their Amharic name, Tissisat, meaning "smoking water." In the past, the spray nourished plentiful vegetation around the waterfalls, but the stark reduction in volume since the hydroelectric plant began operation has lamentably caused most of this plant life to die off. Despite its somewhat reduced state, the Blue Nile Falls is still considered to be one of Ethiopia's most popular tourist attractions, and is quite accessible.

After the falls, the Blue Nile flows west across Ethiopia and then northwest into the Sudan. It joins the White Nile at Khartoum and continues as the mighty Nile River through Egypt, ending in the Mediterranean Sea at Alexandria. The White Nile is the longer river of the two, but the Blue Nile holds the higher volume of water, contributing between 60 and 80 percent of the total intake at Khartoum. Due to the importance of the Nile River to the rise of Egyptian civilization, the quest to discover the source of the Blue Nile has involved such titans of history as Herodotus, Alexander the Great, and Julius Caesar.

Far left: *The Blue Nile Falls have been much altered by the presence of the hydroelectric station, and only occasionally display their former monumentality, but the raging waters still command, and rightly deserve, attention and respect from the onlooker.*

Top right: *The Blue Nile River crashes magnificently over the falls around 18.6 miles (30km) from the city of Bahir Dar, which lies near the southwest corner of Lake Tana.*

Right: *Even with reduced flow the Blue Nile Falls offers one of the most alluring images of the Ethiopian panorama, as the mighty river spreads majestically behind the 147ft (45m) drop.*

LAKE OF MANY ISLANDS

Lake Tana, which gives the river its bulk, is in turn supplied by three rivers: Little Abay, Reb River, and Gumara River. There are 37 islands on the lake, a number of these holy to the Ethiopian church. On the holy islands, 14th-17th century monasteries safeguard the remains of emperors and ancient treasures. The monks of Tana Quirkos believe that the Arc of the Covenant was once kept there. In total, the islands are thought to support a population of around 15,000 people. But it is not only humans who inhabit the lake. Fasilidas Island is an important wetland for local wildlife, and the lake supports a thriving fishing industry. A control weir at the mouth of the Blue Nile now regulates water levels and flow.

Amhara, Ethiopia

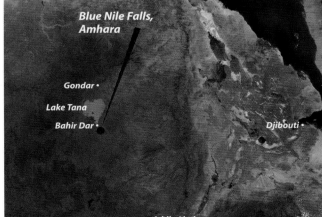

Blue Nile Falls, Amhara

Gondar •

Lake Tana

Bahir Dar •

Djibouti •

• Addis Ababa

Huangguoshu Waterfall

Guizhou Province, China

• **The Huangguoshu Waterfall in western China is the largest waterfall in Asia.**

• **The segmented waterfall is the central attraction of Huangguoshu National Park and is unusual in that it offers visitors the opportunity to experience the falls from behind the curtain of water.**

• **It is said that the sound made by the water as it plunges down the precipitous cliff face can be heard up to 3 miles (5km) away.**

The Huangguoshu National Park is located in a mountainous area around 28 miles (45km) to the southwest of the city of Anshun in Guizhou Province, western China. The Baishui River flows through the park, plunging over no fewer than eighteen waterfalls in the process. The falls vary in size and spectacle, but the most magnificent of them all is the famous Huangguoshu Waterfall.

The waterfall is 316ft (96m) high and 346ft (105m) wide, and in the rainy season, the volume of water flowing over it is such that the cliff actually trembles.

The are several points around the magnificent waterfall where visitors can enjoy the majestic spectacle. Two pavilions situated on the surrounding cliffs provide stunning views, one of them being placed so that it is possible to look down on the falls.

At the bottom of the falls, another pavilion stands at the side of the Rhinocerous Pool, providing a much closer experience of the roaring water. The most exciting and impressive of them all, however, is the Water-Curtain Cave, a 440ft (134m) long undercut behind the falls eroded by the falling water, which is 131ft (40m) above the Rhinocerous Pool. Here visitors can get really close to the curtain of water, even touching it if they wish.

Every year, the park is the venue for the Huangguoshu Waterfall Festival, a series of events aimed at promoting the many tourist attractions of Ghuizhou Province.

Far left: *At the crest of the Huangguoshu Waterfall, the strong flow of the wide river is broken into several distinct arching columns by the projecting rocks of the sheer cliff over which it hurtles.*

Top right: *At the bottom, the thrusting columns of water crash into a 36ft (11m) deep, normally emerald-green plunge pool, known as Xi Niu Tan (Rhinocerous Pool, so called because of its shape), throwing up clouds of spray and foam, which shimmer in the sunlight, often generating rainbows.*

Right: *Visitors can enter the "Shuiliandong," or the Water-Curtain Cave, which runs behind the falls themselves, and offers a unique view of this natural wonder—and the opportunity to reach out and touch the cascading waters.*

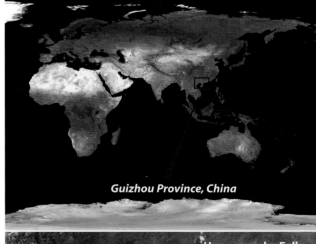

Guizhou Province, China

Huangguoshu Falls, Guizhou Province

Guiyang •

• Kunming

CHINA

Húsavík •

• Nanning

VIETNAM

• Hanoi

A FIRST IMPRESSION
The Huangguoshu Waterfall was discovered in 1683 by the great Ming Dynasty explorer Xu Xiake. On seeing the falls, he remarked, "The sprays burst apart like pearls and jades and the foams rise like a mist… I have seen waterfalls that are much higher and more precipitous, but never a waterfall with such a width and magnificence."

Victoria Falls

Livingstone, Zambia/Zimbabwe

- **Victoria Falls is the widest uninterrupted falls in the world, with an estimated average width of 5,700ft (1,737m).**
- **There are four major portions to the Victoria Falls: The Devil's Cataract, Main Falls, Rainbow Falls, and the Eastern Cataract.**
- **The falls are known locally as "mosi-oa-tunya," which means "the smoke that thunders."**

Victoria Falls may be the most awe-inspiring in the world. The scale of the waterfalls can only be surpassed by Iguaçu. The Zambezi River that feeds Victoria Falls starts off calmly upriver, but by the time it reaches the fracture in the basaltic plateau, it has widened to approximately one mile (1.6km), with small islands scattered along its route. It then plunges in a single drop 350ft (107m), but unlike other falls its flow is arrested by the opposite wall of a deep chasm just 195ft (60m) wide. Under typical conditions, the spray rises to a height of 1,300ft (400m), and is visible from up to 12.4 miles (20km) away. Approximately 120 million gallons (550 million liters) of water gush over the falls every minute.

Victoria Falls is a UNESCO World Heritage Site, and both Zambia and Zimbabwe have responsibility to maintain the integrity of the site. Both countries have a national park and developed tourist facilities, but the increasing political turmoil has led to a drastic drop in visitor numbers to Zimbabwe, and rapid development and environmental issues has prompted calls to withdraw the UNESCO designation.

The two national parks offer the visitor the chance to see plentiful wildlife—typically zebra, giraffes, elephants, baboons, and antelopes. Myriad species of fish and birdlife can also be seen, including 35 species of raptor alone.

Far left: *The falls are unusual in that they are formed along a flat plateau of basaltic lava, not the usual terrain of mountains and valleys. The rocks were formed 200 million years ago, and as they cooled and cracked soft limestone filled in the gaps. The great gorges that collect the water from the falls are a result of the erosion of this softer sediment by the Zambezi.*

Top right: *The erosion of the gorges continues: there are eight such waterfalls in the fractured volcanic tableau, and it is estimated that a ninth set will eventually form at the western end of the falls.*

Right: *During the flood season (February–May), the falls are almost impossible to see. The volume of water and power unleashed during the plunge makes the spray practically impenetrable. The dry season, from September to January, reveals more islands on the Zambezi on the crest of the falls, as the river slows down enough to allow swimming or walking close to the drop in some places.*

Livingstone, Zambia/Zimbabwe, Southern Africa

DAVID LIVINGSTONE

David Livingstone, a Scottish missionary, was exploring the Zambezi River when he discovered Victoria Falls in 1855. He had heard about the immense scale of the falls before he reached the area, but like most Europeans he was sceptical. Livingstone approached the falls with his group in a canoe, but when they saw the great clouds of spray decided to land on an island, now called Livingstone Island, and approach by land. He named the falls after his queen. Livingstone returned five years later to fully explore the area and record his discovery.

Chamarel Falls

Chamarel, Mauritius

Far left: *Not far from Chamarel village the falls plunge from the top into a broad basin, surrounded by lush greenery. The primitive vegetation that proliferates near the waterfall would once have covered the entire island of Mauritius. The little village is well known for its coffee plantations, and the palms that thrive in the area's deer reserve.*

- **This segmented plunge waterfall in the Black River Mountains of Mauritius has a drop of 272ft (83m).**
- **It stands at the confluence of the Saint-Denis River and the River du Cap.**
- **The landscape around the top of the falls is moorland punctuated by outcrops of primeval vegetation.**

Mauritius is an island of volcanic origin that lies in the Indian Ocean around 500 miles (800km) east of Madagascar and 110 miles (177km) northeast of Réunion, on roughly the same latitude as Rio de Janeiro, Brazil. This small but magical island is around 38 miles (61km) long and 29 miles (47km) wide. At its center is a rim of small mountains surrounding a plateau, which may have been the crater of the volcano from which the land first formed.

The highest point on Mauritius, the Petite Rivière–Noire Peak, is 2,711ft (826m) above sea level. From this highland region, powerful rivers flow down steep courses to the ocean. Chamarel Falls stands on one such flow; two of the other main rivers—Grand River South East and Grand River North West—are the island's major sources of hydroelectric power.

Chamarel Falls can be found just inland from the southwestern coast of the island, about 6 miles (10km) south of Tamarin. The village has been developed as a holiday resort that is popular with surfers, and due to the exceptionally high level of sunshine in the district, is also the heart of salt production in Mauritius.

From the village of Case Noyale, a winding road leads to the intriguing colored dunes of Chamarel, and the spectacular Chamarel Falls, which rise from the moors and native plant life in a site of rare natural beauty. There are tourist restaurants in Chamarel village, not far from the falls, where visitors can sample traditional Mauritian cuisine.

Top right: *There are three main segments to the plunge, which plummet 272ft (83m) from the semicircular wall of the basin, which itself is undercut beneath the falls by erosion.*

Right: *The falls are reached via a steep, muddy track. Visitors are advised to keep to the track, since the thick bushes conceal the proximity of the drop. At the top there is a railed platform which affords a stunning view across the valley toward the face of the falls.*

MULTICOLORED SANDS

The area surrounding the Chamarel Falls, known as the Seven-Coloured Earth, is of immense fascination because of its undulating landscape of multicolored sands. The blues, greens, reds, and yellows that appear there were formed by different types of volcanic ash that were deposited in prehistoric times, covered by subsequent sedimentation, and finally exposed again to the surface by wind erosion.

The sands have a peculiar property of settling into distinct layers of their own color caste, even if mixed together. It is not permitted to walk on the sands, which have an eerie, other-worldly quality. The colors can play tricks on the eye so that what appear to be shadows are actually areas of different color.

Chamarel, Mauritius

MAURITIUS

Port Louis

Tamarin

RÉUNION

Chamarel Falls, Mauritius

Maria Cristina Falls

Mindanao, Philippines

• **The Maria Cristina Falls is a cascade on the island of Mindanao in the Philippines.**

• **Its waters are divided into two mighty streams by a great outcrop of rock at its lip. The total drop of the falls is 320ft (98m).**

• **The falls stand on the Agus River. This waterway is short and steep—only 23 miles (36km) from its source in Lanao Lake, 2,200ft (670m) above sea level, to its mouth—and unnavigable, because for much of its length it is rocky and no more than around 4ft (1.2m) deep.**

The Agus River is extremely important economically, because it is fast-flowing—speeds of 30mph (48km/h) are typical—and strong; it has a throughput of around 28,600 gallons (108,262 liters) per second.

The strength of the river has been harnessed by generators along its course, which together supply threequarters of Mindanao's electricity requirements. The most notable of these structures is the Agus VI hydroelectric power plant at the base of the Maria Cristina Falls.

Ninety percent of the falls' waters are used to power the plant. Although the plant is set back around half a mile (800m) from the cascade, the concrete buildings, generators, and security fences have been strongly criticized by environmentalists, although this does little to lessen the appeal of the falls to the thousands of tourists who flock there.

Maria Cristina Falls is one of more than 20 waterfalls within the Iligan City area, a metropolis that owes its development to water power. Because of the large number of falls, Iligan is proudly known as the "City of Majestic Waterfalls."

The city is also the home of numerous nationally acclaimed artists, poets, cultural workers, and writers. Maria Cristina Falls lies just over 5 miles (8km) to the southwest of the downtown area.

Far left: *Pure white plumes of shimmering water—resembling cotton wool—descend with a loud roar from the rim of the falls, separated by a large projecting rock at its center.*

Top right: *The twin plunges crash to the base with immense power, creating a broiling mass of churning mist and spray.*

Right: *The intense beauty of the falls is undeniable, and it is admirable to consider that this body of cascading water is responsible for the creation of vast amounts of electricity—a fascinating and aesthetic phenomenon that is captured for highly practical purposes.*

TRAGIC SISTERS

Traditionally, the falls are named after two almost certainly mythical sisters. One, Maria, threw herself over the precipice because of what she mistakenly believed was her unrequited love for a handsome man. When the other sister, Cristina, learned of Maria's fate, she committed suicide by the same method. The man, who had loved Maria with all his heart, was devastated and buried them both at the base of the falls. He never subsequently married.

Mindanao, Philippines

Cebu city

Maria Cristina Falls, Mindanao

Iligan City

Cotabato City

Davao City

General Santos City

Augrabies Falls

Northern Cape Province, South Africa

• **Augrabies Falls in South Africa is the highest waterfall on the Orange River. A segmented punchbowl formation, it is commonly categorized as the world's sixth largest in terms of volume throughput.**

• **The name of the falls is an Afrikaans corruption of the Khoi name Aukoerebis, meaning "place of great noise."**

• **Below the Augrabies Falls, the Orange River drops another 1,000ft (300m) over the next 5.5 miles (9km) in a series of smaller waterfalls and rapids.**

After a lazy and largely uneventful course for around 75 miles (120km) across the Northern Cape from Upington, the Orange River leaves its granite plateau and tumbles into a huge sheer-sided gorge that extends for the next 11 miles (18km) downstream.

The Augrabies Falls that mark this transition first appeared around 500 million years ago when the plateau was formed by upheavals deep beneath the surface of the Earth.

As the river prepares to leave the plateau, it divides itself into numerous channels which turn to rapids before taking the plunge.

The total drop is around 625ft (191m), while the main cascade falls 183ft (55.7m). The horizontal extent of the rapids varies according to season—at their height in summer (December–February), they stretch for several miles and lead into 19 separate waterfalls. However, the principal cascade never carries less than 80 percent of the total flow.

During peak flood years, which occur on average around once every decade, the flow of water is more than 2 million gallons (9 million liters) per second. At such times, the falls are almost submerged by the waters below, which can reach a depth of 500ft (152m).

Far left: *The plunge pool is like a gigantic basin hewn from the rock face, deep and inaccessible. From here the raging waters discharge into a deep gorge that runs for 11 miles (18km).*

Top right: *In this dramatic view of the falls—a similar angle to that shown far left—the extensive floodwater has spilled over the higher level rock formations and has virtually filled the vast pool with a violent surge of silt-carrying water.*

Right: *Further on in the falls' rapid and noisy run the water squeezes between tightly enclosed cliff faces, spewing out in a broad cascade and filling yet another pool.*

POOL OF MYSTERY

The plunge pool at the base of the Augrabies Falls is 300ft (92m) across and probably around 427ft (130m) deep. It is almost completely inaccessible, even in the dry season. Often, it cannot be seen at all through the great mass of spray. That has given rise to several legends, most famously that it contains a mass of alluvial diamonds, washed downstream over millions of years and deposited in the still-water swirl hole at the bottom. Another story is that within the uncharted depths is the lair of a hideous snakelike monster.

Northern Cape Province, South Africa

Augrabies Falls, Northern Cape Province

• Upington

Beaufort West •

Cape Town •

INDEX

ACKNOWLEDGMENTS

Corbis: Cover, main, bottom left; 11 right; 20; 21 bottom; 46; 52; 60; 62; 76; 77 top, bottom; 78; 84; 89 bottom; 91 top; 93 top; 102; 108; 109 top; 132; 134; 135 top; 144; 146; 147 bottom; 148; 157 top, bottom.

Getty Images: 28; 32; 55 top; 89 top; 93 bottom; 95 bottom; 97 bottom; 103 bottom; 105 bottom; 111 bottom; 117 bottom; 119 top; 130; 131 bottom; 149 bottom; 151 bottom.

Photolibrary: 4; 10; 12; 13 top; 26; 36; 37 top; 53 bottom; 54; 56; 58; 64; 65 top; 68; 70; 80; 82; 83 bottom; 86; 87 bottom; 88; 90; 92; 94; 96; 104; 105 top; 110; 116; 117 top; 118; 121; 124; 126; 128; 142; 152; 156.

iStockphoto: Cover, bottom center/Nitin Sanil, bottom right/Harald Fischer, back/Jason Maehl; 6/Naphtalina; 7 right/Jonathan Chambers, below right/Patricia Hofmeester; 9 right/Ken Brown; 16/Mike Norton; 17 top/David Crowther; 18/Ashok Rodrigues; 19 top/Christoph Achenbach, bottom/Arnar Valdimarsson; 21 bottom/Vera Bogaerts; 22/Linda & Colin McKie; 23 top/Sherrianne Talon, bottom/Steve Graafmans; 24/Prozone235; 27 top/Matthew Antonino, bottom/Sebastian Schäfer; 29 top, bottom/Sergey Korotkov; 33 bottom/Miloš Mokotar; 34/Bruce Becker; 35 top/Karen Massier, bottom/Lisa Kyle Young; 37 bottom/Oliver Isermann; 38/Eldon Griffin; 39 top/Michael Madsen, bottom/Anton Foltin; 40/Cathleen Abers-Kimball; 41 top/Andre Nantel, bottom/Alexander Kolomietz; 42/Alexander Hafemann; 43 top/Maxime Vige; 44/Gabriela Schaufelberger; 45 top/Matthias Wassermann; 49/Deborah Benbrook; 51 bottom/Andrew Coleman; 57 top, bottom/Murat Baysan; 59 bottom/Joe Gough; 63 top/Pat Bonish, bottom/Julio Yeste; 66/Maxime Vige; 67 top/Zsolt Biczó, bottom/DWPhotos; 69 top/Rod Stafford; 71 top/Lucia Busnello, bottom/Matteo Mazzoni; 72/Sander Kamp; 73 top, bottom/Rognar; 81 bottom/Stuart Blyth; 85 bottom/Waldemar Wellmann; 100/Harald Fischer; 101 top/Paolo Porcellana; 103 top/Ray Roper; 107 bottom/Sia Yambasu; 111 top/Ling Xia; 112/Björn Kindler; 113 top, bottom/BMPix; 114, 115 top/Janine White; 115 bottom/Jack Thornton; 120/Gary Forsyth; 121 top/Andrew Barker; 122, 123 top, bottom/Moonet; 125 top/Laurin Johnson; 127 top/Ashok Rodrigues; 133 top/Cosmopol, bottom/Torsten Karock; 137 bottom/Johan Keijzer; 138, 139 bottom/Marco Manzini; 140/Eva Browning; 141 top/Lisa Devlin; 143 top/Gary Muth; 147 top/Barkley Fahnestock; 151 top/James Scully; 153 top/John Woodworth, bottom/Ken Sorrie; 154, 155 top, bottom/FlemishDreams.

Fotolia: 9 top/J. Hindman; 11 top/Ang M.C.; 31 bottom/Nathan Jaskowiak; 33 top/JKaczka Digital Imaging; 50, 51 top/Oksana Perkins; 81 top/Tom Curtis; 106/Paula Cobleigh; 107 top/Rimasz; 109 bottom/Urosr; 136/Muehle; 137 top/Stepan Jezek; 143 bottom/Jodie Johnson; 150/Patalpin.

Wikimedia Commons: Cover, spine/Tom Keene; 7 top/Yosemite; 8/Walter Siegmund; 17 bottom/Moondigger; 25; 30/Urban; 31 top/Stan Shebs; 43 top/Simon Cole; 45 bottom/Satmap; 47 top/merlinthewizard, bottom/Sorenriise; 48/Roger McLassus; 49 bottom/Tryggvi Aðalbjörnsson; 53 top/Alejandro Rodriguez; 55 bottom/Andreas Tille; 59/Amos T. Fairchild; 65 bottom/Breakyunit; 69 bottom/Mick Knapton; 75; 79 top/Ruben Lohaus Brito; 79 bottom; 83; 85/Kierano; 87 top/rh; 91 bottom/Bobyfume; 95 top/Tom Keene; 97 top/Jensbn; 99 bottom/Qyd; 119 bottom/Didier B; 125; 127/Clemensfranz; 129 top/Docmarton, bottom/Rrevanuri; 131 top/JShook; 139 top/Arun Prasad; 141/Ewok Slayer; 145 top, bottom/AMG; 149 top/WaitinZ.

Sachin Rai: 7 bottom right.

Jared Smith: 13 bottom.

Chris Poulton: 14, 15 top, bottom.

Martin Hunter: 21 top.

Brendan Marris: 25 bottom.

Dino D'Ambrosio: 61 top, bottom.

Danny Wayte & Thomas Woodstone: 74, 75 bottom respectively.

Northwest Waterfall Survey: 98, 99 top/Bryan Swan.

Ken Douglas: 101 bottom.

Amnon Itchah: 135 bottom.

NASA Visible Earth: All satellite images.

Every effort has been made to contact the copyright holders for images reproduced in this book. The publishers would welcome any errors or omissions being brought to their attention.